THE PASSOVER AND FEAST OF UNLEAVENED BREAD

Workbook

Passover & Feast of Unleavened Bread Workbook

All rights reserved. By purchasing this Activity Book, the buyer is permitted to copy the activity sheets for personal and classroom use only, but not for commercial resale. With the exception of the above, this Activity Book may not be reproduced in whole or in part in any manner without written permission of the publisher.

Bible Pathway Adventures® is a trademark of BPA Publishing Ltd.
Defenders of the Faith® is a trademark of BPA Publishing Ltd.

ISBN: 978-1-98-858596-3

Author: Pip Reid

Creative Director: Curtis Reid

For more Bible resources, including workbooks and printables, visit our website at:

www.biblepathwayadventures.com

◇◇ Introduction ◇◇

Welcome to the Passover & Feast of Unleavened Bread Biblical Studies Workbook. This 8-week curriculum includes eight ready-to-use lesson plans and a variety of hands-on activities designed to help students explore Passover and the Feast of Unleavened Bread (Pesach and Chag HaMatzot) in a fun and engaging way. Through these lessons, students discover the significance of the Spring Appointed Times and their place within the history of the House of Israel.

Inside, you'll find clear Scripture references for easy Bible study, along with a complete answer key for guidance and clarity. Gather your supplies and prepare to guide students through the events and meaning of the Passover and Feast of Unleavened Bread.

Bible Pathway Adventures helps parents and educators teach children the biblical faith in a fun and engaging way through workbooks, printable resources, and illustrated Bible stories, available at www.biblepathwayadventures.com.

The search for Truth is more fun than Tradition!

◇• Table of Contents •◇

Introduction 3
How to Use This Book 8
The Appointed Times 9

Lesson One: Let My people go! 11
Lesson plan: Let My people go! 12
Worksheet: Hebrew slaves in Egypt 14
Map activity: Where is Egypt? 15
Worksheet: Who was Moses? 16
Worksheet: Let My people go! 17
Coloring page: Out of slavery 18
Bible quiz: Let My people go! 19
Math worksheet: Plagues math challenge 20
Worksheet: Decode the hieroglyphics 21
Role-play worksheet: Plagues of Egypt 22
Worksheet: Yah's plague power 23
Story sequencing activity: Plagues of Egypt 24
Worksheet: Land of Goshen 25
Creative writing: Hebrews in the land of Goshen 26
Worksheet: Light in Goshen 27
Let's learn Hebrew: Mosheh 28

Lesson Two: The First Passover 31
Lesson plan: The First Passover 32
Bible activity: The Hebrew calendar 34
Worksheet: Yah's instructions for Israel 35
Worksheet: Let's inspect the lamb! 36
Coloring page: The Passover 37
Worksheet: Protected by the blood 38
Did you know? Blood of the lamb 39
Let's learn Hebrew: Pesach 40
Worksheet: A Passover meal 42
Worksheet: A Passover invitation 43
Bible quiz: The first Passover 44
Bible puzzle: The Feast of Unleavened Bread 45
Worksheet: Feast of Unleavened Bread 46
Recipe: Let's make matzah! 47
Let's learn Hebrew: Matzah 48

Bible word search puzzle: Feast of Unleavened Bread 50
Creative writing: The Exodus escape 51
Worksheet: The Exodus begins 52
Coloring page: Leaving Egypt... 53

Lesson Three: The Last Supper **55**
Lesson plan: The Last Supper 56
Worksheet: Feast of Unleavened Bread 58
Worksheet: Triumphal Entry 59
Worksheet: Interview a disciple 60
Comic worksheet: Cleansing the Temple 61
Bible quiz: The Last Supper 62
Bible word search puzzle: The Master's last meal 63
What's the Word: Blood of the Covenant 64
Coloring page: Do this in remembrance of Me 65
Worksheet: The upper room 66
Bible word unscramble: The twelve disciples 67
Worksheet: Yeshua and the Twelve 68
Worksheet: Steps of Discipleship 69
Bible puzzle: A renewed commandment 70
Worksheet: Final instructions 71
Creative writing: Write a story 72

Lesson Four: Betrayal of the King **73**
Lesson plan: Betrayal of the King 74
Worksheet: Yah's Appointed Times 76
Worksheet: Sabbath to Sukkot 77
Bible story worksheet: Betrayal of the king 78
Worksheet: 30 pieces of silver 79
Did you know? worksheet: Judas' betrayal 80
Worksheet: Freedom from Roman rule 81
Bible quiz: Garden of Gethsemane 82
Worksheet: Betrayal in the garden 83
Worksheet: Watch and pray 84
Worksheet: Yeshua on trial 85
Worksheet: Before the Sanhedrin 86
Worksheet: Caiaphas, the high priest 87
Story sequencing activity: Sequence the story 88
Math worksheet: Unleavened math challenge 89
Let's learn Hebrew: Feast of Unleavened Bread 90
Worksheet: Preparation Day in Jerusalem 92
Worksheet: Preparation Day chart 93

Lesson Five: The Crucifixion 95
Lesson plan: The Crucifixion 96
Coloring worksheet: Yeshua before Pilate 98
Bible crossword puzzle: Pontius Pilate 99
Coloring page: Walking to Golgotha 100
Worksheet: Journey to Golgotha 101
Newspaper worksheet: The Jerusalem Times 102
Coloring worksheet: Your Passover meal 103
Worksheet: The Passover Lamb 104
Bible quiz: The Crucifixion 105
Creative writing: The Crucifixion 106
Worksheet: Betrayal and the cross 107
Worksheet: The Passover meal 108
Worksheet: Into the tomb 109
Coloring page: Into the tomb 110
Worksheet: Passover in Jerusalem 111
Bible quiz: Feast of Unleavened Bread 112
Coloring worksheet: The centurion's statement 113

Lesson Six: He is Risen! 115
Lesson plan: He is Risen! 116
Worksheet: First of the firstfruits 118
Worksheet: Sheaf of the firstfruits 119
Coloring page: The sheaf of the firstfruits 120
Bible word search puzzle: He is risen! 121
Let's learn Hebrew: Bikkurim 122
Creative writing: Firstfruits in Jerusalem 124
Worksheet: Altar of burnt offering 125
Coloring worksheet: The guards report 126
Worksheet: Bribing the guards 127
Worksheet: Did you know? 128
Coloring page: The saints 129
Bible crossword puzzle: The cross and empty tomb 130
Map activity: From doubt to belief 131
Bible quiz: The resurrection 132
Worksheet: Timeline to resurrection 133

Crafts & Projects
Bible craft: Yah's covenant 135
Bible craft: Create your own Passover lamb 139
Bible craft: The last supper 143
Bible craft: Make a Passover banner 147
Bible craft: Temple treasures 151
Certificate of Achievement 157

Lesson Materials Checklists 159

Answer Key 166
Discover more Workbooks! 174

How to Use this BOOK

The *Passover & Feast of Unleavened Bread Workbook* guides students through the events surrounding the first Passover and Feast of Unleavened Bread and their fulfillment in Jerusalem thousands of years later. It follows the historical sequence recorded in the Torah, beginning in Exodus with the Ten Plagues and the first Passover in the land of Egypt, when the Israelites were protected by the blood of the lamb. In Lessons One and Two, students explore Yah's instructions to the Israelites, the first Passover meal, and the events that led to the Exodus from Egypt.

Lessons Three through Six take place in Jerusalem during the days leading up to the Feast of Unleavened Bread, when Yeshua entered the city on a young donkey. Students examine Yeshua's last supper with His disciples, His betrayal in the Garden of Gethsemane, the trial before the Sanhedrin, the crucifixion, and His burial, and how these events unfolded alongside Passover preparations in Jerusalem. The workbook concludes with the discovery of the empty tomb and the Firstfruits Ceremony, demonstrating how Yeshua's resurrection took place in fulfillment of Yah's Spring Appointed Times.

Each lesson includes a ready-to-use lesson plan supported by worksheets, Bible puzzles, creative writing activities, crafts, maps, and coloring pages. Clear learning objectives and key Scripture references help students understand both the historical events recorded in the Torah and their fulfillment in the life, death, and resurrection of Yeshua.

The Appointed TIMES

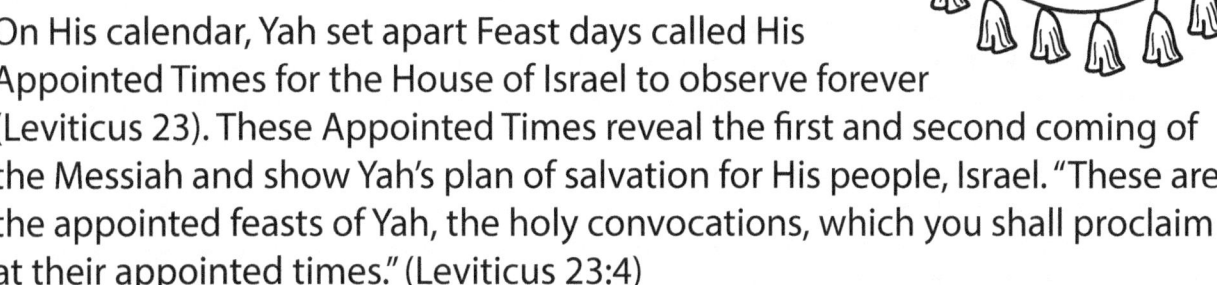

On His calendar, Yah set apart Feast days called His Appointed Times for the House of Israel to observe forever (Leviticus 23). These Appointed Times reveal the first and second coming of the Messiah and show Yah's plan of salvation for His people, Israel. "These are the appointed feasts of Yah, the holy convocations, which you shall proclaim at their appointed times." (Leviticus 23:4)

The Spring Feasts include the Feast of Unleavened Bread, which begins with the Passover meal. During this meal, we remember how Yah delivered the Hebrews from slavery in the land of Egypt and how Yeshua fulfilled this Appointed Time through His death on the cross at Golgotha thousands of years later. During this Feast, we also remember how the Hebrews left Egypt with unleavened bread and how it reminds us today to remove spiritual leaven from our lives. This Feast also points to Yeshua's resurrection on the day of firstfruits in Jerusalem. Shavu'ot (Pentecost) celebrated 50 days later, reminds us of the giving of the Torah at Mount Sinai and the giving of the Holy Spirit in Jerusalem (Acts 2).

These Feasts were given to the ancient Israelites who were brought out of Egypt. They remain to this day for His people in the scattered House of Israel. They help us see how Yeshua the Messiah fulfilled the Scriptures through His death and brought them to life through His resurrection. Through Him, we have the power of the Ru'ach (Holy Spirit) to this day, so that these may become the living Spring Appointed Times in our lives.

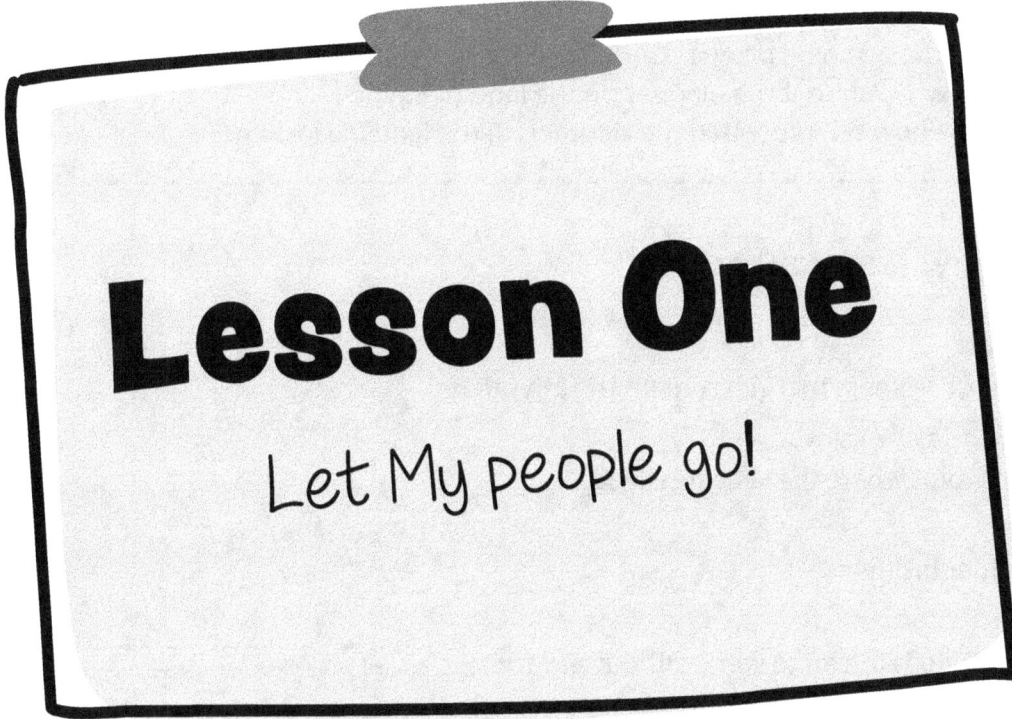

Lesson One

Let My people go!

Lesson Plan for: Let My people go!
Exodus 5:1-11:10

1. Lesson objectives:

During this lesson, students will:
* Identify the first nine plagues that Yah sent upon the land of Egypt.
* Explain why Yah sent the plagues on the land of Egypt.
* Describe how Yah protected the Hebrews in the land of Goshen.

2. Review key vocabulary:

- **PLAGUE:**
  A disaster or sickness that Yah sent on the Egyptians.
- **LAND OF GOSHEN:**
  A part of Egypt where the Israelites lived.
- **AARON:**
  Moses' older brother.
- **SLAVE:**
  Someone who is forced to work without pay for someone else.
- **PHARAOH:**
  The ruler of Egypt who refused to obey Yah and let the Israelites go.

3. Bible memory verse:

"I will send all My plagues on you, your servants and your people so that you may know that there is none like Me in all the earth." (Exodus 9:14)

Did you know?

Yah sent the plagues to show that the gods of Egypt had no power compared to Him. (Numbers 33:4)

Object lesson idea

Show students a soft sponge and a hard rock. Let them squeeze the sponge and touch the rock and explain that Pharaoh's heart became hard when he refused to obey God, even after seeing many powerful signs. Just as the rock does not change when squeezed, Pharaoh would not change his heart.

4. Read Exodus 5:1-11:10 or read the Bible story below:

The Hebrews had lived in Egypt as slaves for many years and were forced to work hard under Pharaoh's rule. Yah chose a man named Moses from the tribe of Levi to lead His people out of slavery. After calling Moses to speak on His behalf, Moses and his brother Aaron went to Pharaoh, the king of Egypt. They said, "Yah, the God of Israel, says, 'Let My people go so they may hold a feast to Me in the wilderness.'" Pharaoh refused and made the Hebrews' work even harder. He ordered them to make bricks without providing straw. They had to gather their own straw while still making the same number of bricks as before. Moses felt discouraged, but Yah reminded him of His covenant with Abraham, Isaac, and Jacob. He promised to bring the Israelites out of Egypt and lead them to the Promised Land. Then Yah revealed His power by sending plagues upon Egypt. The Nile River turned to blood, and frogs covered the land. Gnats and swarms of flies followed, but Yah protected the Hebrews living in Goshen. A deadly disease struck the livestock, painful boils appeared on the people, and fiery hail destroyed crops and trees. Locusts ate what remained, and thick darkness covered Egypt for three days. Each plague showed that Egypt's false gods had no power. Still, Pharaoh refused to free the Hebrews. Finally, Moses warned him that the firstborn in every Egyptian household would die. Even then, Pharaoh would not let the children of Israel go.

5. Let's discuss:

1. What was today's Bible story about?
2. Why did Moses and Aaron go to Pharaoh?
3. How did Pharaoh respond to God's command?
4. Why did God send plagues on the land of Egypt?
5. Can you name the first nine plagues?
6. Where did the Hebrews live during the plagues?
7. How did God protect the Hebrews from the plagues?
8. Why do you think Yah hardened Pharaoh's heart?

6. Activities:

* Worksheet: Hebrew slaves in Egypt
* Map activity: Where is Egypt?
* Worksheet: Who was Moses?
* Worksheet: Let My people go!
* Bible craft: Yah's covenant
* Coloring page: Out of slavery
* Bible quiz: Let My people go!
* Math worksheet: Plagues math challenge
* Worksheet: Decode the hieroglyphics

* Role-play worksheet: Plagues of Egypt
* Worksheet: Yah's plague power
* Story sequencing activity: Plagues of Egypt
* Worksheet: Land of Goshen
* Creative writing: Hebrews in the land of Goshen
* Worksheet: Light in Goshen
* Let's learn Hebrew: Mosheh

Hebrew slaves in Egypt

After Joseph brought his family to the land of Egypt during the great famine, the Hebrews lived peacefully for many years. Joseph had saved Egypt by storing grain, and Pharaoh rewarded him by giving his family land in Goshen. But after Joseph died, another Pharaoh rose to power who did not remember all that Joseph had done for Egypt. Read Exodus 1:1-22 and the article below, then answer the questions.

This Pharaoh noticed that the Hebrew people were growing in number and strength. He feared they might join Egypt's enemies in war, so he made them slaves. The Egyptians forced the Hebrews to build cities such as Pithom and Raamses. They worked long hours making bricks and carrying heavy stones. Pharaoh treated them harshly, but Yah blessed the Hebrews and their families continued to grow.

Pharaoh then ordered the midwives to kill all the Hebrew baby boys at birth, but they feared Yah and refused. So, Pharaoh commanded that every Hebrew baby boy be thrown into the Nile River. One Hebrew mother hid her baby in a basket and placed him among the reeds along the riverbank. Pharaoh's daughter found the child and named him Moses, which means "drawn out of the water." Years later, Yah spoke to Moses from a burning bush in Midian and told him to return to Egypt. Through Moses, he would lead His people out of slavery and set them free.

Answer the questions below.

Why did Pharaoh make the Hebrews slaves in Egypt?

What did Pharaoh command the midwives to do to the Hebrew baby boys?

How did one Hebrew mother save her child?

Where is Egypt?

The Hebrews lived and worked in the land of Egypt for many years before Yah freed them from slavery (Exodus 1-12). Where was Egypt located? Use an atlas or a reliable internet source to find and draw the country of Egypt on the map below.

- ☐ Find and mark the land of Egypt in green.
- ☐ What countries or regions are near Egypt?
- ☐ What kind of land or climate does Egypt have?

Describe how Pharaoh treated the Hebrews in the land of Egypt.

....

....

....

Who was Moses?

Read Exodus 2:1-4:31 and complete the worksheet below.

Who adopted Moses?
....
....

Moses fled to the land of Midian because:
....
....

God's powerful signs to Moses (Exodus 4):
....
....
....

God sent Moses back to the land of Egypt to:
....
....

Moses had two sons: .... and ....

From the story you just read, write five words that describe Moses:

① ....
② ....
③ ....
④ ....
⑤ ....

Let My people go!

Moses and Aaron went to Pharaoh and asked him to let the children of Israel go (Exodus 5:1–2). How did Pharaoh respond? Write their conversation in the speech bubbles above. Then, write below how Pharaoh made life harder for the Hebrews.

....
....
....
....

Let My PEOPLE GO!

Read Exodus 5:1-11:10. Answer the questions below.

1. Who did Yah send to speak to Pharaoh, the king of Egypt?
2. What message did Moses and Aaron give to Pharaoh from Yah?
3. How did Pharaoh respond when Yah told him to let the Hebrews go?
4. What did Pharaoh do to make the Hebrews work harder?
5. Why did God send plagues on the land of Egypt?
6. What was the first plague God sent?
7. Where did the Hebrews live during the plagues?
8. In Exodus 6, what covenant did God remind Moses of?
9. What warning did Moses give Pharaoh about the final plague?
10. What did Yah promise to do for the Hebrews if they followed His instructions?

Plagues Math Challenge!

(Based on Exodus 7-12)

Directions: Solve each math problem below. Show your work in the boxes.

1 River of Blood

When Yah turned the Nile River to blood, it lasted for 7 days. If each day the Egyptians used 20 jars of water from other sources, how many jars did they use in total during that time?

2 Plague of Frogs

During the second plague, frogs covered the land. If one frog laid 200 eggs, and 15 frogs were near a single home, how many eggs might they lay altogether?

3 Fiery Hail

When Yah sent hail upon the land of Egypt, it destroyed 800 fields of grain. Each field had 125 bundles of wheat. How many bundles were destroyed in all?

Decode the HIEROGLYPHICS

"Moses and Aaron went to Pharaoh and did just as Yah commanded. Aaron cast down his staff before Pharaoh and his servants, and it became a serpent. Then Pharaoh summoned the wise men and the sorcerers, and they, the magicians of Egypt, also did the same by their secret arts. For each man cast down his staff, and they became serpents. But Aaron's staff swallowed up their staffs. Still Pharaoh's heart was hardened, and he would not listen to them, as Yah had said."
(Exodus 7:10-13).

a	𓅀	h	□	o	🪢	v	🐍
b	👢	i	⟨	p	▢	w	🦅
c	⌒	j	〰	q	◣	x	⌒⌒
d	⌬	k	⌣	r	⬭	y	⟨⟨
e	⟨⟨	l	🦁	s	▯	z	▭
f	🐍	m	🦉	t	⌒		
g	⌂	n	〜	u	🐦		

**Who did Yah say He would bring out of Egypt?
Use the ancient Egyptian alphabet to decode the answer.**

....
children   of   Israel

✱ Read Exodus 7:14-9:35. Where were the Hebrews safe from the plagues? Why do you think Yah continued to harden Pharaoh's heart?

Role-play challenge

Yah sent Moses and Aaron to Pharaoh with a message: "Let My people go!" Each time Pharaoh refused, Yah sent another plague upon Egypt to show His power. Read Exodus 5:1-11:10, then work with your friends, family, or classmates to act out these events from the Bible.

Choose A Role:

Each card has a prompt to help you start your lines. Circle the role you will play.

Prompt: "Yah says, 'Let My people go!'" — MOSES

Prompt: "Pharaoh, Yah has sent a sign to show His power." — AARON

Prompt: "I will not let the Hebrews go!" — PHARAOH

Prompt: "Don't you yet know that Egypt is destroyed?" — SERVANT

Write Your Script:

Write three sentences your character might speak.

1. ....
2. ....
3. ....

Act It Out:

Work together to act out one or more of the plagues e.g. frogs hopping everywhere, fiery hail falling from the sky, or darkness covering the land. Be creative! Use green pom-poms or toy frogs for the plague of frogs, red, orange, and yellow tissue paper for fiery hail, and flashlights or dark sheets for the plague of darkness.

Yah's plague power

Read Exodus 7:19-10:23. In each plague, Yah gave Moses a command to begin the plague, and Moses later acted when Yah caused the plague to stop. Write Yah's command that started certain plagues and Moses' action that stopped them in the empty boxes below.

Yahweh Says START	Moses STOPS IT

Plague of Blood

Plague of Frogs

Plague of Gnats

Plague of Flies

Plague of Darkness

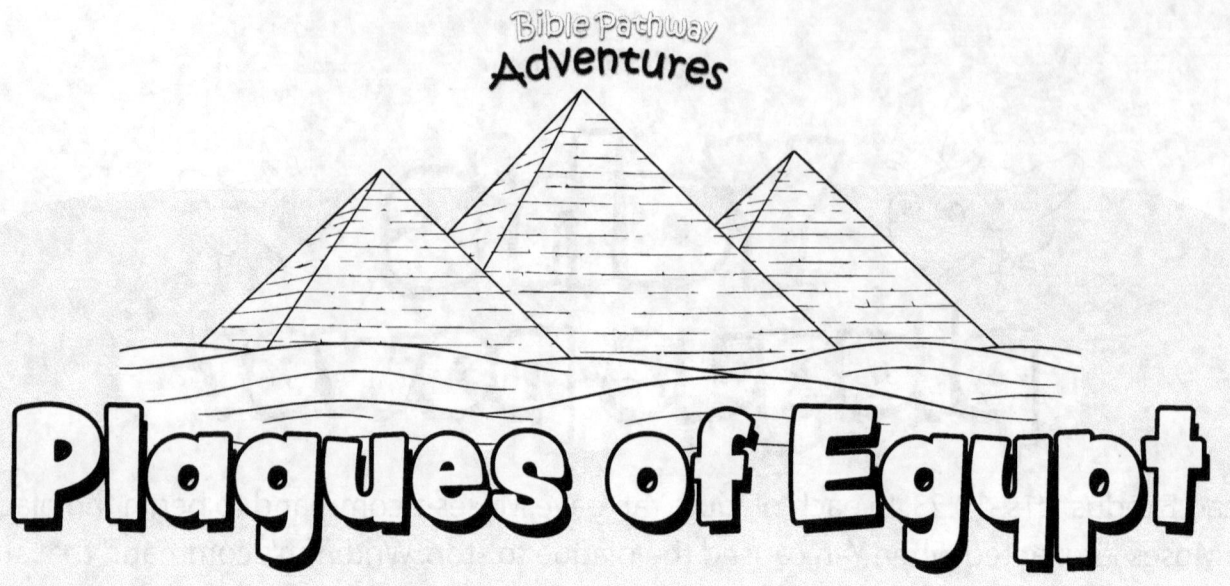

Plagues of Egypt

Read Exodus 5:1-11:10 and review the nine sentences below. They recount the story of the first nine plagues, but they're out of order! Your task is to arrange the sentences correctly. Write a number next to each sentence to sequence the events in their proper order.

A. .... A plague brought sickness to the Egyptian animals, but the Hebrews' animals were unharmed.

B. .... Yahweh decided to send ten plagues to show His power over Pharaoh and the Egyptian gods.

C. .... Pharaoh made the Hebrews work harder by forcing them to find their own straw for bricks.

D. .... The second plague brought frogs everywhere, filling the Egyptians' homes.

E. .... God sent lice and flies, causing trouble throughout Egypt.

F. .... Another plague covered Egypt in darkness for three days, but the Hebrews had light in the land of Goshen.

G. .... Moses and Aaron told Pharaoh that God said to let the Hebrews go, but Pharaoh refused.

H. .... The first plague turned the Nile River into blood, killing the fish and making the water undrinkable.

I. .... God sent boils, hail with fire, and locusts to ruin Egypt's crops and health.

Land of Goshen

When Yah sent His plagues on Egypt, the land of Goshen, where the Hebrews lived, was kept safe. When Yah sent flies, they did not enter Goshen. During the plague on livestock, none of the Hebrews' animals died. When darkness covered Egypt for three days, the Hebrews in Goshen still had light in their homes. Read Genesis 46-47 and Exodus 8-9. Where was the land of Goshen? Mark it on the map and then answer the questions below.

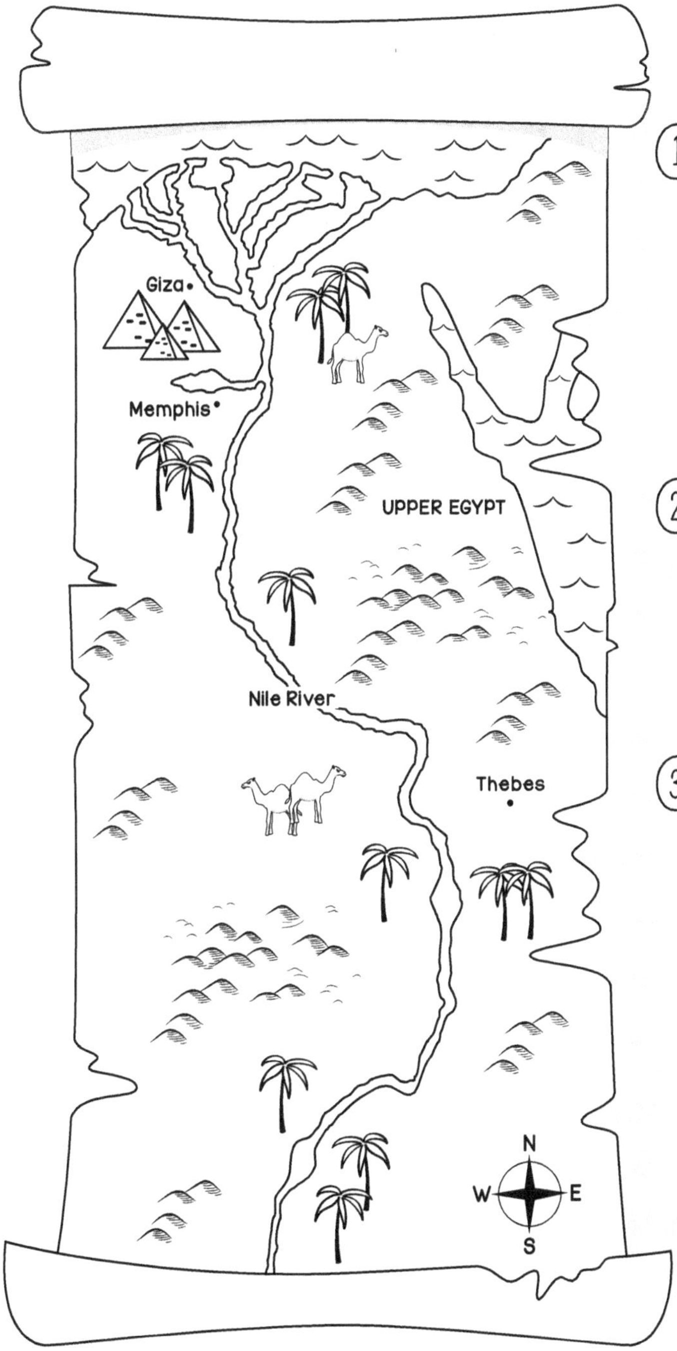

1) Read Genesis 46. Why were the Hebrews living in the land of Goshen?

....
....
....

2) What did the Hebrews do in the land of Goshen?

....
....

3) Name three Bible verses that mention the land of Goshen:

....
....
....
....
....

Write a letter

Imagine you are a Hebrew living in the land of Goshen while the plagues are happening. Write a letter to a friend about how Yah protected your family and what you heard or saw happening to the Egyptians nearby.

....
....
....
....
....
....
....
....
....
....

Light in Goshen

Read Exodus 10:21-29. During the ninth plague, Yah covered Egypt with darkness for three days. The darkness was so thick that the Egyptians could not see one another or leave their homes, but the people of Israel in Goshen still had light. On the left side of your page, draw Egypt covered in darkness. On the right side, draw Goshen, where the Israelites lived in light.

LAND OF EGYPT

LAND OF GOSHEN

"The Egyptians did not see one another, nor did anyone rise from his place for three days, but all the people of Israel had light where they lived." (Exodus 10:23)

Mosheh

The Hebrew name for Moses is Mosheh. Moses was from the tribe of Levi, one of the twelve tribes of Israel. When he was born, Pharaoh had ordered all Hebrew baby boys to be killed. To save him, Moses' mother placed him in a basket by the river. Pharaoh's daughter found him and raised him as her own son in the palace. When Moses grew up, he saw an Egyptian hurting a Hebrew slave and defended him, killing the Egyptian. Moses fled to the land of Midian, where he became a shepherd. One day, God spoke to Moses from a burning bush and told him to lead the Israelites out of Egypt. Moses was unsure, but God promised to be with him and sent his brother Aaron to help.

Mosheh
(Moh-SHEH)

מֹשֶׁה

Moses

Trace the Hebrew name here:

Write the Hebrew name here:

Let's write!

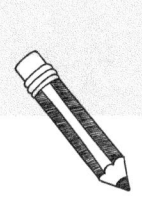 Practice writing 'Mosheh' on the lines below.

משה

משה

Try this on your own.
Remember that Hebrew is read from RIGHT to LEFT.

How do you think Moses' experience growing up in Pharaoh's palace and later living as a shepherd prepared him to lead the Israelites out of Egypt?

Lesson Two

The First Passover

Lesson Plan for: The First Passover
Exodus 12:1-13:16

1. Lesson objectives:

During this lesson, students will:
* Explain how obeying Yah's instructions protected the Israelites during the final plague.
* Recall key details of the first Passover meal and the Feast of Unleavened Bread.
* Learn how Yah commanded the Israelites to remember the Passover and the Feast of Unleavened Bread each year.

2. Review key vocabulary:

- **THE PASSOVER MEAL:** A meal of lamb, bread, and bitter herbs.
- **LAMB:** A young sheep.
- **DOORPOSTS and LINTEL:** The sides and top of a doorway where the lamb's blood was placed.
- **FIRSTBORN:** The oldest child in a family.
- **UNLEAVENED BREAD:** Bread made without yeast, also known as MATZAH.

3. Bible memory verse:

"When I see the blood, I will pass over you, and no plague will befall you to destroy you…" (Exodus 12:13)

Did you know?

Unleavened bread is bread made without yeast. It is usually made from ingredients such as flour and water, and sometimes salt. The Israelites ate unleavened bread because they had to leave Egypt quickly and did not have time to let their dough rise.

Object lesson idea

Show a picture of a doorframe. Explain that the Israelites obeyed Yah by placing blood on the doorposts and lintel of their homes. In this way, they were protected from the final plague. How does the blood of the lamb protect you today?

4. Read Exodus 12:1-13:16 or read the Bible story below:

After Yah had sent nine plagues on Egypt, Pharaoh still refused to let the Israelites go. Yah said to Moses, "I will bring one more plague upon Egypt. After that, Pharaoh will let you go." As this final plague approached, Yah gave Moses and Aaron new instructions. He told Moses that this month would become the first month of Israel's year. On the tenth day of the month, each family was to select a perfect, one-year-old male lamb. The lamb was to be kept until the fourteenth day of the month. On that evening, the Israelites were to kill their lambs at twilight, roast the meat, and eat it with unleavened bread and bitter herbs. They were to eat in haste, dressed and ready to leave, with their belts fastened, sandals on their feet, and staffs in their hands. Yah also commanded the Israelites to place the lamb's blood on the doorposts and lintel of their homes. The blood would be a sign of protection, because Yah was about to bring the tenth plague upon Egypt. At midnight, Yah passed through Egypt, and every firstborn died, from Pharaoh's household to the animals. But Yah passed over the homes marked with blood and kept the Israelites safe. After this, Pharaoh ordered them to leave Egypt at once. They left quickly, carrying unleavened dough because there was no time for it to rise. Yah then told them to remember this event each year by keeping Passover and the Feast of Unleavened Bread. During this Feast, they were to remove all leaven from their homes and eat unleavened bread for seven days, remembering how Yah brought them out of slavery with a mighty hand.

5. Let's discuss:

1. What was today's Bible story about?
2. What type of lamb did Yah tell each family to choose, and what happened on the fourteenth day?
3. Why was the lamb's blood placed on the doorposts and lintel of the houses?
4. How did Yah protect the Israelites during the final plague?
5. Why were the Israelites told to eat the Passover meal in haste?
6. Why did the Israelites leave Egypt with silver, gold jewelry, and clothing?
7. What is the Feast of Unleavened Bread?
8. When the Israelites entered the land of the Canaanites, what were they told to teach their children?

6. Activities:

- Bible activity: The Hebrew calendar
- Worksheet: Yah's instructions for Israel
- Worksheet: Let's inspect the lamb!
- Coloring page: The Passover
- Worksheet: Protected by the blood
- Did you know? Blood of the lamb
- Let's learn Hebrew: Pesach
- Worksheet: A Passover meal
- Worksheet: A Passover invitation
- Bible craft: Create your own Passover lamb
- Bible quiz: The first Passover
- Bible puzzle: The Feast of Unleavened Bread
- Worksheet: Feast of Unleavened Bread
- Recipe: Let's make matzah!
- Let's learn Hebrew: Matzah
- Bible word search puzzle: Feast of Unleavened Bread
- Creative writing: The Exodus escape
- Worksheet: The Exodus begins
- Coloring page: Leaving Egypt…

The Hebrew calendar

Exodus 12 and the Hebrew calendar

In Exodus 12:1, God spoke to Moses and Aaron while they were in Egypt. He said, "This month will be the beginning of months for you. It will be the first month of your year." In Hebrew culture, the first month of the year was called Nisan. It usually occurred around March or April.

Your Task: Finish writing the names of the Gregorian (modern) months below the Hebrew months below. Then, in the empty space under each month, draw fruits, vegetables, or plants that grow in your country during that time of year.

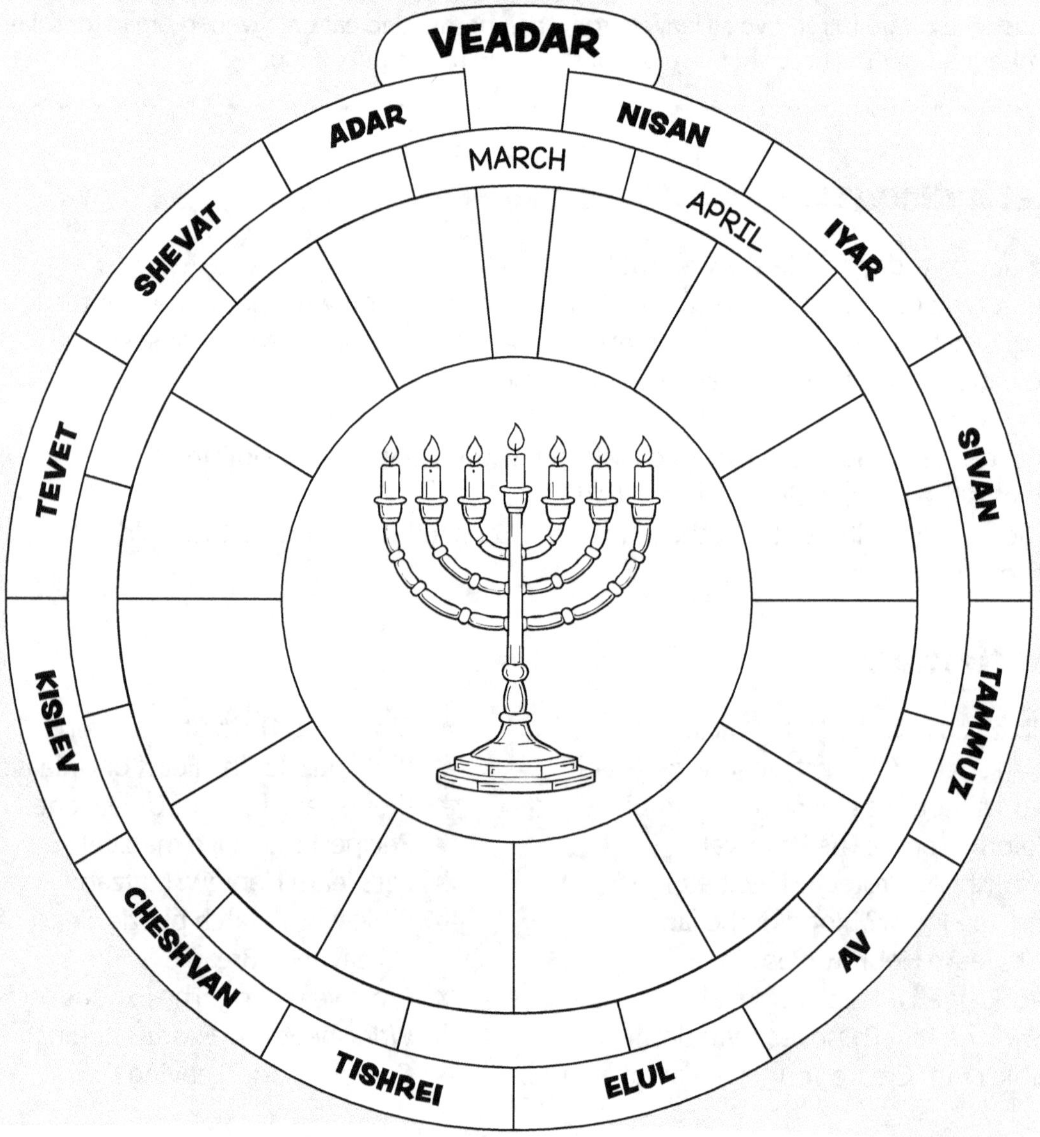

Hebrew months (outer ring): VEADAR, ADAR, NISAN, IYAR, SIVAN, TAMMUZ, AV, ELUL, TISHREI, CHESHVAN, KISLEV, TEVET, SHEVAT

Gregorian months filled in: MARCH (under Adar), APRIL (under Nisan)

Yah's Instructions for ISRAEL

Read Exodus 12:1-16. Yah gave the Israelites instructions for their first Passover meal in the land of Egypt. Write in each box what these instructions were.

PASSOVER FOOD	CHOOSING THE LAMB	MARKING WITH BLOOD	EATING THE MEAL

 **Discuss: How did obeying these instructions protect the Israelites?**

Let's inspect the lamb!

When Yah prepared to rescue the Israelites from the land of Egypt, He gave Moses and Aaron instructions for the first Passover meal. On the tenth day of the month, each Israelite family had to choose one lamb or young goat for their household. The animal had to be a one-year-old male without defect. The Israelites were to keep it until the fourteenth day of the month and then sacrifice it at twilight. The blood of this animal would protect them when Yah passed through Egypt and struck down the firstborn. Read Exodus 12:1-14 and then complete the worksheet below.

✓ **Check the correct boxes that show it meets the Passover rules.**

- ☐ Is too old
- ☐ No defects at all
- ☐ Is a male
- ☐ Has spots
- ☐ Has a torn ear
- ☐ One-year-old

Why is it important to follow Yah's instructions?

....
....
....
....

Draw a blemish on me that would disqualify me from being a Passover lamb.

---

www.biblepathwayadventures.com
Passover & Feast of Unleavened Bread Workbook

© BPA Publishing Ltd 2025

"...When I see the blood, I will pass over you..."

(Exodus 12:13)

Protected by the Blood

During the first Passover in the land of Egypt, Yah told the Israelites to mark their doors with the blood of a spotless lamb or goat. This act of faith protected their families when He passed through Egypt and struck down the firstborn in the land (Exodus 12:1-23). Follow the instructions below to represent the blood the Israelites placed on the doorposts and lintels of their homes.

What you'll need:

 A small twig or leafy branch (for making your hyssop brush).

 String or thread (to tie the leaves or grass).

 A small bowl or paper plate.

 Red acrylic craft paint.

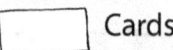 Cardstock.

Instructions:

1. **Make your brush:** Find a twig or leafy branch. Tie a few leaves or soft grass to one end with string or thread to make a hyssop-style brush.
2. **Cut the strips:** Cut a piece of cardstock into long strips. These strips will represent the blood placed on the two doorposts and the top beam of the doorway.
3. **Paint the strips:** Pour some red acrylic craft paint into a bowl. Dip your twig brush into the paint and spread it across each strip of cardstock. Set the strips aside and allow them to dry.
4. **Place on the doorway:** Attach the painted strips to both sides of the doorway and across the top beam.

Did You Know?

The blood of the first Passover lambs saved Israelite lives in Egypt. In Exodus 12, Yah told the Israelites to brush the lamb's blood on the doorposts and lintels of their homes. When He passed through the land of Egypt at midnight, the homes marked with blood were spared from death. Thousands of years later, Yeshua fulfilled this Appointed Time in Jerusalem. At the ninth hour (3p.m.), as Temple priests killed the Passover lambs on the afternoon of Nisan 14, Yeshua cried out and gave up His spirit (Mark 15:33-37).

Draw an Israelite brushing the lamb's blood on the doorposts and lintel of their home.

Pesach

The Hebrew name for Passover is Pesach. Before the Israelites left Egypt, they ate a meal of lamb, unleavened bread, and bitter herbs. This meal was part of God's plan to protect them from the final plague. God asked the Israelites to remember and honor this Appointed Time forever (Exodus 12:14). Each year, they were to observe the Passover meal to remind them of how God delivered them from slavery in Egypt and brought them to freedom. Later, Yeshua was crucified outside the city of Jerusalem during Passover.

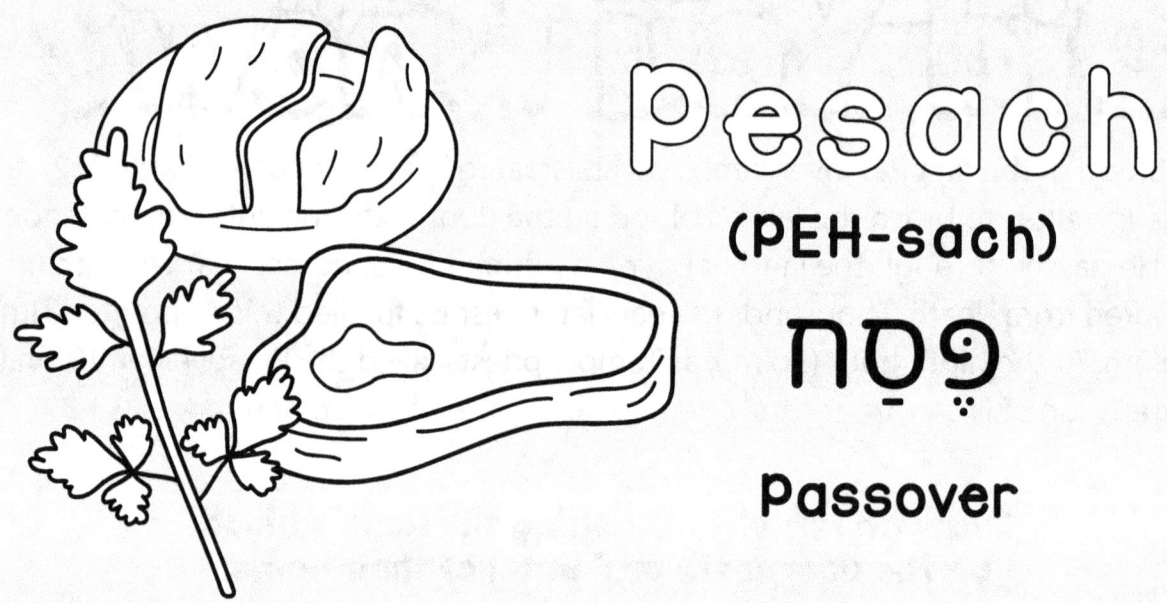

Pesach (PEH-sach)

פֶּסַח

Passover

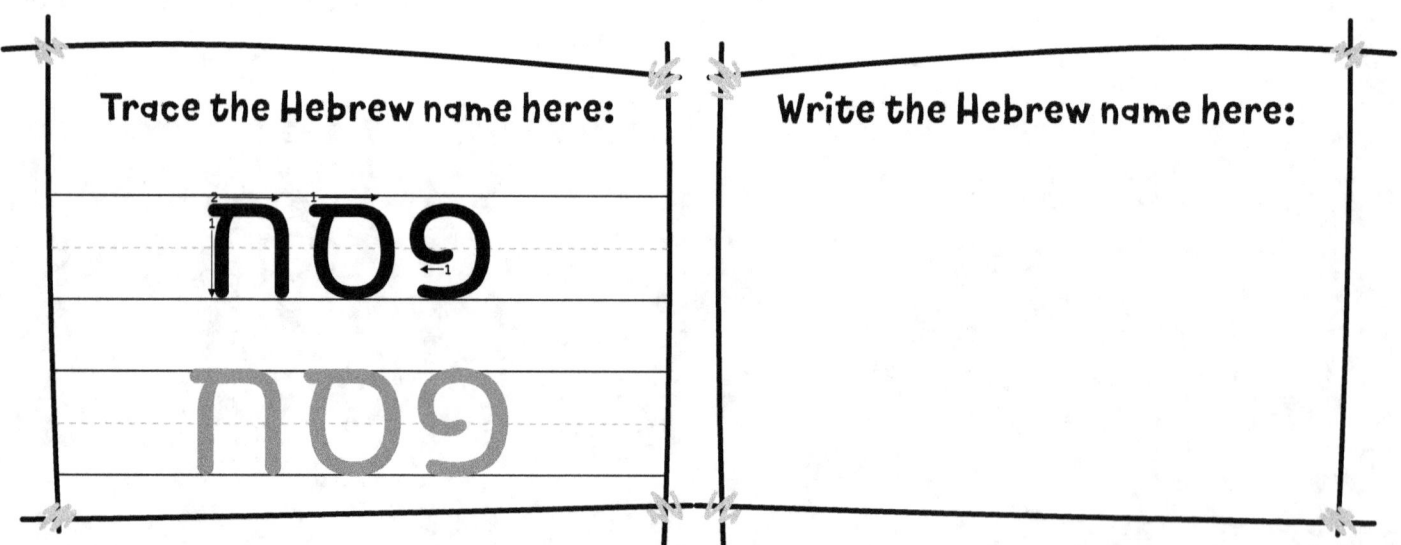

Trace the Hebrew name here:

Write the Hebrew name here:

Let's write!

Practice writing 'Pesach' on the lines below.

פסח

פסח

Try this on your own.
Remember that Hebrew is read from RIGHT to LEFT.

Read Exodus 12:1-28. Why do you think God told the Israelites to eat the Passover meal quickly?

....
....
....
....

A Passover meal

When the Israelites were in Egypt, they ate their first Passover meal. What food did they eat? Read Exodus 12:1-11 to find the three foods that God asked His people to eat in haste, with their cloak tucked into their belt, their sandals on their feet, and their staff in their hand. Draw each food in the empty sections on your plate. Next to each drawing, write what the food helps you remember today. When you are finished, color your plate!

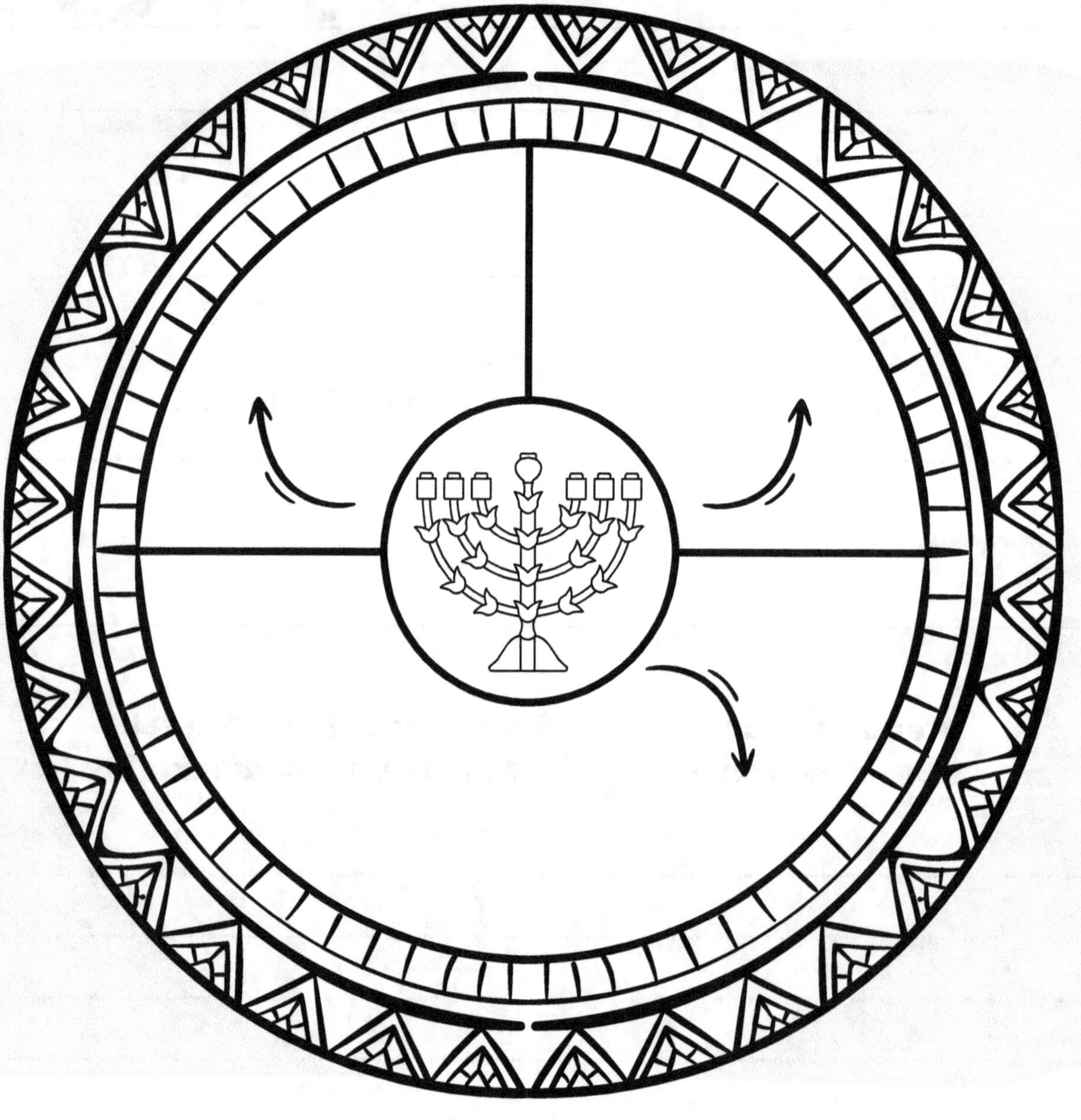

Imagine you are an Israelite living in ancient Egypt during the days leading up to the final plague. Moses has just told everyone that Yah has given special instructions for this night. Each household must prepare a meal with lamb, unleavened bread, and bitter herbs, and mark their doorposts with the lamb's blood for protection. Read Exodus 12 and complete the worksheet below. When you're done, discuss why Yah gave the Israelites such specific instructions.

THE PASSOVER MEAL

YAH'S INSTRUCTIONS

HOW WOULD I GET READY?

WHAT WOULD I EAT?

Read Exodus 12:1-51. Answer the questions below.

1. What did God tell the Israelites to do to protect themselves during the final plague?

2. What animal were the Israelites told to sacrifice for the Passover?

3. Where did the Israelites put the blood of the lamb?

4. What would the blood on the doorposts protect the Israelites from?

5. What special meal did the Israelites eat on the night of Passover?

6. How long did God tell the Israelites to observe the Feast of Unleavened Bread?

7. What food were the Israelites told not to eat during the Feast of Unleavened Bread?

8. What happened to the firstborn in every Egyptian household during the final plague?

9. What did Pharaoh say after the final plague?

10. What did the Israelites do after Pharaoh told them they could leave Egypt?

Feast of Unleavened Bread

Read Exodus 12:1–20. Yah told the Israelites to observe the Feast of Unleavened Bread for seven days, throughout their generations, forever. What special food did He tell them to eat each day during this Appointed Time? Each number represents a letter of the alphabet. Substitute each number with a letter to reveal the words.

A	B	C	D	E	F	G	H	I	J	K	L	M
1	2	3	4	5	6	7	8	9	10	11	12	13

N	O	P	Q	R	S	T	U	V	W	X	Y	Z
14	15	16	17	18	19	20	21	22	23	24	25	26

1) 19 – 5 – 22 – 5 – 14:

2) 4 – 1 – 25 – 19:

3) 25 – 15 – 21:

4) 19 – 8 – 1 – 12 – 12:

5) 5 – 1 – 20:

6) 21 – 14 – 12 – 5 – 1 – 22 – 5 – 14 – 5 – 4:

7) 2 – 18 – 5 – 1 – 4:

Feast of Unleavened Bread

The Feast of Unleavened Bread is one of Yah's Appointed Times (Leviticus 23) and has been celebrated for thousands of years. It began when Yah freed the Israelites from slavery in Egypt, as told in Exodus 12. He told them to leave quickly, so they made bread without yeast, called unleavened bread, because there was not enough time to let it rise. In their hurry, the Israelites also took their dough that had not risen yet, along with their kneading bowls. This Feast lasts for seven days and begins with the Passover meal.

Centuries later, Israelites from many places traveled to Jerusalem to worship at the Temple during this Feast. Before the Feast of Unleavened Bread, Yeshua came to Jerusalem and rode in on a donkey. The Israelites cheered and hoped He would be their king and save them from the Romans. But Yah had a different plan. While the Israelites were eating their Passover meal, remembering the lamb's blood that saved them in Egypt, Yeshua was crucified outside the city. He became the ultimate Passover Lamb, taking away the sins of the world, as it says in John 1:29: "Behold, the Lamb of God, who takes away the sin of the world."

1. What is unleavened bread, and why did the Israelites make it when they left Egypt?

2. Why do you think Yah wanted the Israelites to leave Egypt so quickly?

3. Why do you think Yah told the Israelites to eat bread without yeast during this Feast?

Let's make Matzah!

INGREDIENTS
1 cup all-purpose flour
1/3 cup vegetable oil
1/8 tsp salt
1/3 cup of water

Prep time: 5 min

Bake time: 8 - 10 min

Tools: Bowl, spoon, fork, parchment paper, baking tray

METHOD
1. Line a baking sheet with parchment paper.
2. Mix the flour, oil, and salt together in a bowl.
3. Add the water and mix until the dough is soft.
4. Using your hands, form the dough into six balls and press them into flat disks on the prepared baking sheet.
5. Use a fork to poke holes across the surface of each disk.
6. Bake at 425°F (220°C) for 8-10 minutes, or until the bread is cooked through.

Did you know?
Matzah reminds us of the Exodus! The Israelites left Egypt in such a hurry that they didn't have time to let their bread rise.

Matzah

The Hebrew name for unleavened bread is matzah. Matzah is a type of bread made from flour and water. It is eaten during one of Yah's Appointed Times, the Feast of Unleavened Bread, to remind the Israelites of the time when they had to leave Egypt in such a hurry that their bread did not have time to rise. During the Feast of Unleavened Bread, matzah is to be eaten each day for seven days as a reminder of this event. To make matzah, you mix flour and water, roll the dough out very thin, and bake it quickly. Since it does not contain yeast, it stays flat and crispy. How do you make matzah during the Feast of Unleavened Bread?

Matzah
(Mah-TSAH)

מַצָּה

Unleavened bread

Trace the Hebrew name here:

Write the Hebrew name here:

Let's write!

Practice writing the Hebrew name for unleavened bread on the lines below.

מצה

מצה

Try this on your own.
Remember that Hebrew is read from RIGHT to LEFT.

Why do you think it's important for Israelites to eat matzah during the Feast of Unleavened Bread?

....
....
....
....

Feast of Unleavened BREAD

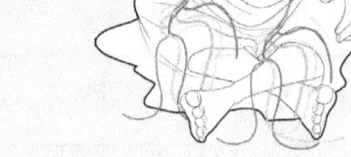

Read Exodus 12:1-51. Find and circle the words below.

```
A U D W Z Y R F V Y M A D D
R P N X J E O A I L R A A W C
W X P L L I P P H B P T I E O
A O O O E D K U F W W Z S L N
X O B I I A Y Z E B E A E L G
E V S H S N V T W U T H V I R
J D E R Z R T E X Z L Q E N E
X K R S A D D E N Q O H N G G
W I V Z P H U X D E K U D P A
Q Q E K H K E F S T D F A L T
E G Y P T K X E U P I S Y A I
F O R E V E R A Z H P M S C O
C M D L P H B S G V Y H E E N
V H N N O K T T V G M L D A R
D Y V I S R A E L I T E S Z C
```

DWELLING PLACE
FEAST
EGYPT
FOREVER
CONGREGATION
MATZAH
OBSERVE
YAHWEH
ISRAELITES
UNLEAVENED
SEVEN DAYS
APPOINTED TIME

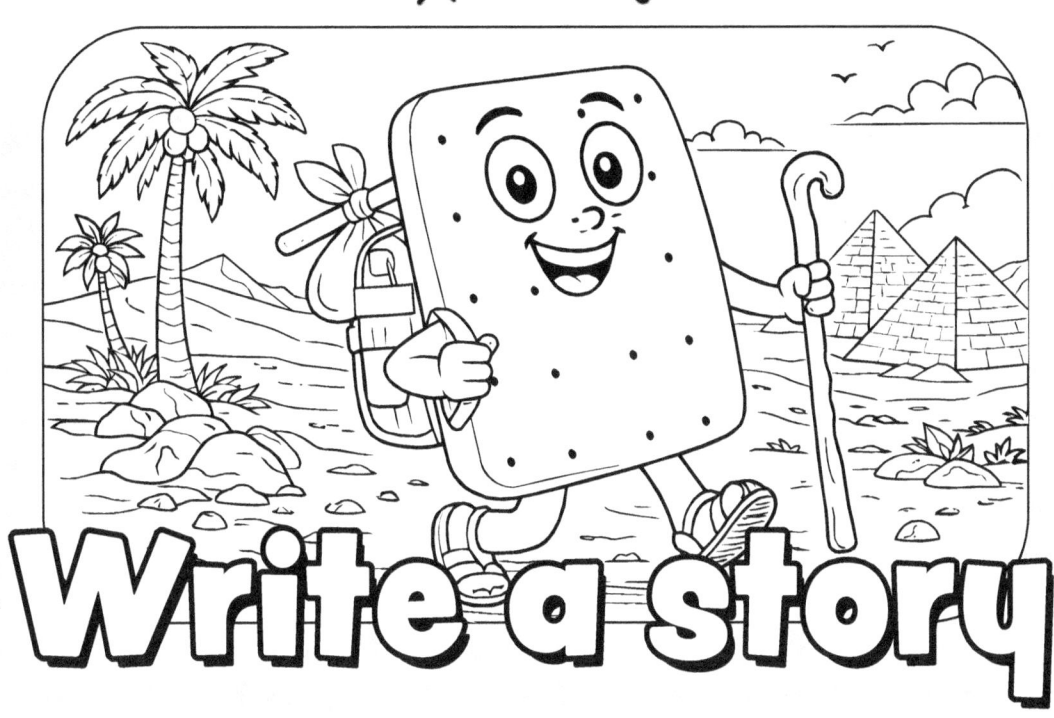

Write a story

Read Exodus 12:1-13:16. Imagine you were an Israelite living in Egypt when Yah set you free from slavery. What did you take with you? How did you feel? Write a story about what it was like to leave Egypt quickly and follow Moses into the wilderness.

....

....

....

....

....

....

....

....

....

The Exodus begins

At midnight, Yah struck down all the firstborn in the land of Egypt, so Pharaoh commanded the Israelites to leave at once. The people of Israel journeyed from Rameses to Succoth, about 600,000 men on foot, besides women, children, and a mixed multitude with their flocks and herds. Read Exodus 12:29-42 and write or draw what the people took with them when they left Egypt.

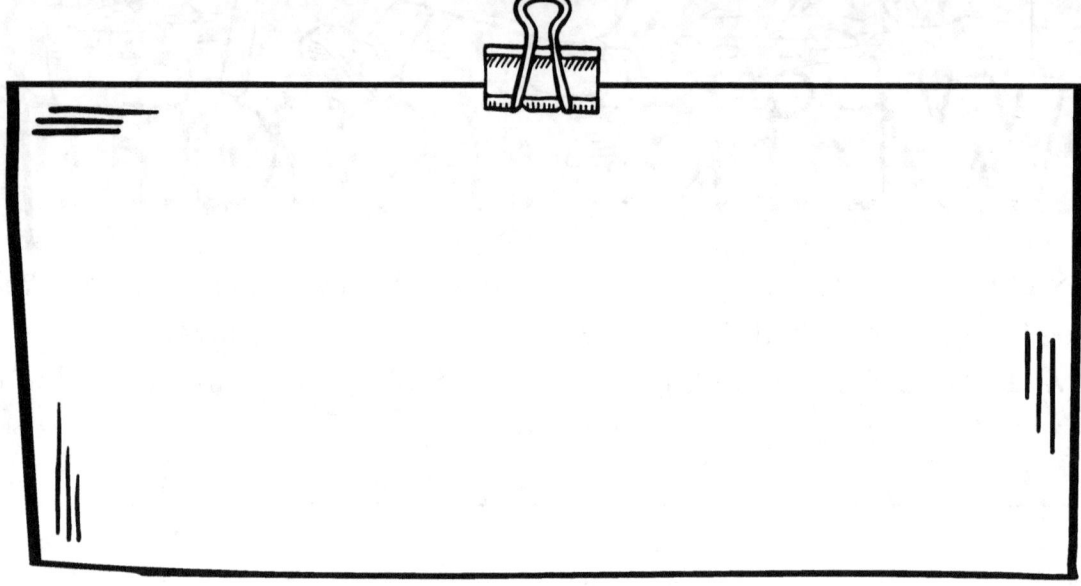

Answer the questions below.

What happened at midnight in Egypt that caused Pharaoh to finally let the Israelites go?

What did the Israelites take with them when they left Egypt?

Who do you think was among the mixed multitude?

Lesson Three
The Last Supper

Bible Pathway Adventures

Lesson Plan for: The Last Supper

Exodus 12-14, Leviticus 23, Matthew 21, 26, Mark 11, Luke 19, 22, and John 12-18

1. Lesson objectives:

During this lesson, students will:
* Identify the key events of Yeshua's final days in Jerusalem, including His triumphal entry.
* Explain why Yeshua cleansed the Temple and shared the Last Supper.
* Explain how the Israelites prepared for the Feast of Unleavened Bread and Passover.

2. Review key vocabulary:

○ TEMPLE:
A large building in Jerusalem where the Israelites worshipped Yah.

○ FEAST OF UNLEAVENED BREAD:
A seven-day Appointed Time, when Israel ate unleavened bread to remember leaving Egypt.

○ DISCIPLE:
A follower and student of Yeshua who learned from His teachings and example.

○ SERVANT:
A person who humbly serves others; Yeshua showed this by washing His disciples' feet.

○ PASSOVER MEAL:
A meal of lamb, unleavened bread, and bitter herbs.

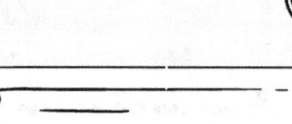

Object lesson idea

Bring two pieces of bread: one leavened and one unleavened. Explain that leaven made bread rise, but during the Feast of Unleavened Bread, the Israelites removed leaven from their homes. This reminded them that they had left Egypt quickly.

3. Bible memory verse:

"A new commandment I give you, that you love one another: just as I have loved you…" (John 13:34)

Did you know?

The ancient Jewish historian Flavius Josephus claimed that more than 2 million people gathered in Jerusalem for one Feast of Unleavened Bread in the first century AD. (Jewish War: Book 6, Chapter 9)

 **4. Read Matthew 21-26; Mark 11-14; Luke 19-22; John 12-18, or read the Bible story below:**

As the Feast of Unleavened Bread drew near, Yeshua traveled to Jerusalem. Many Israelites had come to the city to keep the Feast, and the streets were crowded as families prepared for Passover. When Yeshua entered the city riding on a young donkey, the crowds were filled with excitement. They welcomed Him with joy, waving palm branches and praising Yah. They called out that Yeshua was the King who comes in Yah's name. The chief priests and scribes, however, were not pleased and began planning how to get rid of Him. After entering the city, Yeshua went to the Temple. It was busy as priests and worshipers prepared for the sacrifices. When He saw money changers and traders using the Temple courts for business, He said, "This is a house of prayer, not a place of greed," and drove them out. A few days later, Yeshua shared a final meal with His disciples to prepare them for what was coming. As they reclined together, He took bread, gave thanks to Yah, broke it, and said, "Take and eat; this is My body." Then He took a cup, gave thanks, and said, "Drink from it, all of you. This is My blood, poured out for many." During the meal, Yeshua told them that one of them would betray Him, and later that night Judas slipped out into the darkness to speak with the chief priests. That same evening, Yeshua wrapped a towel around Himself and washed His disciples' feet, setting an example for them to follow. He gave them a new commandment: to love one another as He had loved them, so that others would know they were His disciples. After teaching and praying, Yeshua left with His disciples and crossed the Kidron Valley to a garden called Gethsemane.

 **5. Let's discuss:**

1. What was today's Bible story about?
2. Why did many Israelites travel to Jerusalem during this time of the year?
3. How did the Israelites welcome Yeshua when He entered Jerusalem?
4. Why were the chief priests and scribes worried about Yeshua?
5. What did Yeshua see happening in the Temple, and what did He do?
6. Why do you think Yeshua shared a final meal with His disciples?
7. What example did Yeshua set when He washed His disciples' feet?
8. What new commandment did Yeshua give His disciples?

 6. Activities:

- Worksheet: Feast of Unleavened Bread
- Worksheet: Triumphal Entry
- Worksheet: Interview a disciple
- Comic worksheet: Cleansing the Temple
- Bible quiz: The Last Supper
- Bible word search puzzle: The Master's last meal
- What's the Word: Blood of the Covenant
- Coloring page: Do this in remembrance of Me
- Worksheet: The upper room
- Bible word unscramble: The twelve disciples
- Worksheet: Yeshua and the Twelve
- Worksheet: Steps of Discipleship
- Bible puzzle: A renewed commandment
- Worksheet: Final instructions
- Creative writing: Write a story
- Bible craft: The last supper

The Feast of Unleavened Bread

During the time of Yeshua, the Feast of Unleavened Bread was one of Yah's pilgrimage Feasts, also called Appointed Times. Each spring, Israelites from the land of Israel and surrounding nations traveled to Jerusalem to celebrate this seven-day Feast. This included people from the scattered House of Israel. Both the Torah and the ancient Jewish historian Flavius Josephus explain that the Feast began at sunset on the fourteenth day of Nisan, right after the Passover lambs were sacrificed and eaten. Josephus wrote that special sacrifices were offered at the Temple every day during the Feast. Priests presented bulls, rams, and lambs along with grain offerings. Smoke from the sacrifices filled the air as families gathered to worship, pray, and share sacred meals. During this time, Israelite families were commanded to eat only unleavened bread and to remove all yeast from their homes.

While the Feast was taking place, Jerusalem became very crowded and busy. Josephus said that a great number of people came from many places. Some pilgrims camped in tents on nearby hills, while others stayed in homes opened to travelers. The narrow streets were filled with prayers, market noise, and the sound of people walking toward the Temple. At the center of the city stood the Second Temple, where priests dressed in white linen served and incense rose into the sky as worshippers bowed in prayer. Roman soldiers watched the crowds from the Antonia Fortress to keep order. Josephus reported that in some years, more than three million people gathered in Jerusalem during the Feast. (Wars of the Jews, Book 6, Chapter 9).

Imagine you are staying in Jerusalem during the Feast of Unleavened Bread. Draw or write what you see as you walk through the city.

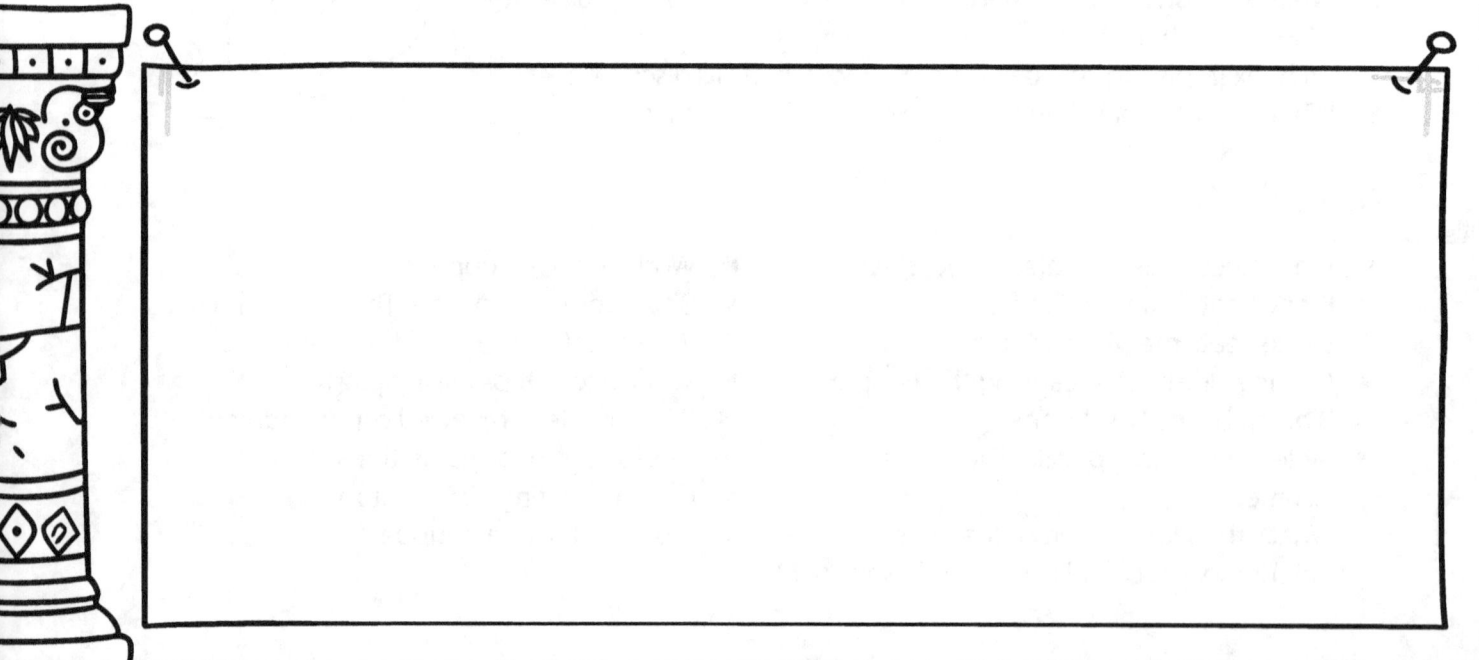

Triumphal Entry

It was the time leading up to the Feast of Unleavened Bread. Jerusalem was crowded with pilgrims arriving for the Feast, and families were busy preparing for Passover. As one of the pilgrimage Feasts commanded in the Torah, Yeshua and His disciples were also traveling to Jerusalem. When they came near the village of Bethphage on the tenth day of the month of Nisan, Yeshua sent two disciples ahead to find a young donkey and its colt and bring them to Him. This was the same day the Israelites, in obedience to Exodus 12:3, selected their Passover lambs and brought them into their homes. The lambs were kept until the fourteenth day of the month.

As Yeshua rode the donkey toward Jerusalem, a crowd that had heard He was coming rushed out to meet Him. "It's the Messiah!" they cried. Many believed He had come to rescue Israel and overthrow the Roman rulers. Waving palm branches, they shouted, "Baruch Haba Be'shem Adonai!" A group of disciples ran ahead, praising Yah with loud voices. "Blessed is the King who comes!" they proclaimed. People spread their cloaks and palm branches on the road, creating a royal path to welcome Him. Some of the Pharisees in the crowd grew angry and said, "Teacher, tell your disciples to be quiet!" But Yeshua answered, "I tell you, if they keep silent, the very stones will cry out!" More people poured out of the city to see what was happening. "Who is this man?" they asked. The crowd replied, "This is Yeshua, the prophet from Nazareth in Galilee."

Read Zechariah 9, Matthew 21, and Luke 19. Answer the questions.

1. Why did Yeshua send two of His disciples into the village?

2. What prophecy came true when Yeshua rode into Jerusalem on a donkey?

3. How did the Israelites welcome Yeshua?

Interview a disciple

Imagine you are one of Yeshua's twelve disciples walking beside Him as He entered the city of Jerusalem (Matthew 21). A magazine has sent you a questionnaire about this incredible day! Tell them about yourself, and describe what you saw, heard, and felt as the crowds shouted, "Blessed is He who comes in the name of Yah!"

1. Introduce yourself.

....
....

2. How long have you been a disciple of Yeshua?

....
....
....

3. Why are you traveling to Jerusalem?

....
....

4. How will you honor the Passover meal?

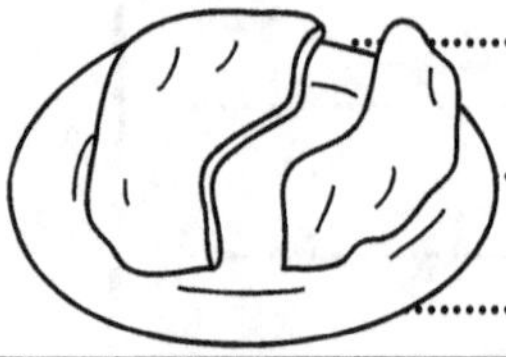

....
....

Cleansing the Temple

Read Matthew 21:12-13 and John 2:13-17 to learn what happened when Yeshua entered the Temple in Jerusalem before the Passover. The Temple was meant to be a house of prayer, but Yeshua found merchants and money changers taking advantage of the people. In each panel, draw what happened to show one of the main events from this story.

CHAOS IN THE TEMPLE

YESHUA STEPS IN

TABLES OVERTURNED

THE PRIESTS ARE ANGRY! A SECRET PLAN TAKES SHAPE.

The Last SUPPER

Read Matthew 26:1-56, Luke 22:1-53, and John 13:1-18:24. Answer the questions below.

1. Where did Yeshua eat a meal with His disciples before His arrest?

2. What did Yeshua and His disciples eat and drink at the meal?

3. Whose feet did Yeshua wash?

4. Which disciple left the meal to betray Yeshua?

5. What new commandment did Yeshua give His disciples?

6. Who did Yeshua say would deny Him?

7. What dispute arose among the disciples?

8. What will we do if we love the Messiah? (John 14:15)

9. Who did Yeshua say will teach us all things?

10. Where did Yeshua take the disciples after the meal?

The Master's LAST MEAL

**Read Matthew 26:1-56, Luke 22:1-53, and John 13:1-18:24.
Find and circle the words below.**

```
Z B C T Q D Y Z G D O B U C K
L H C I F E O E A W N O X U O
Q J Y A E A R H S I T D S P R
J U D A S W T A A H M Y Z O C
J K O W S I S H S W U T Z R O
B L O O D L M R E E N A Y J M
K H F Y S V R S M R O M Q T M
S E M N M Y L S K I K J E G A
Z C O V E N A N T A N N U K N
M W S Q P G W K N X A F W W D
E B D G D Q D H N J L P V P M
U P P E R R O O M Y V O Z I E
B R E A D F M F G W F Y E N N
V G M M D I S C I P L E S P T
C G L W A S H F E E T S G K D
```

COVENANT
BLOOD
BREAD
UPPER ROOM
COMMANDMENT
BODY
JUDAS
FATHER
DISCIPLES
WASH FEET
YESHUA
CUP

Blood of the Covenant

Read Mark 14:12-25. Using the words below, fill in the blanks to complete the Bible passage. Then discuss whether this meal was a Passover meal or simply a final meal share by Yeshua and His disciples. What do you think, and why?

UNLEAVENED	PASSOVER	BETRAYS	KINGDOM	BREAD
DISCIPLES	CUP	BLOOD	COVENANT	MASTER

"On the first day of the Feast of .... Bread, when it was customary to sacrifice the Passover lamb, Yeshua's disciples asked Him, "Where do you want us to go and make preparations for you to eat the Passover?" He sent two of His ...., telling them, "Go into the city, and a man carrying a jar of water will meet you. Follow him. Say to the owner of the house he enters, 'The .... asks: Where is my guest room, where I may eat the .... with My disciples?' He will show you a large room upstairs, furnished and ready. Make preparations for us there." The disciples left, went into the city and found things just as Yeshua had told them, and prepared the Passover. When evening came, Yeshua arrived with the Twelve. While they were reclining at the table eating, He said, "Truly I tell you, one of you will betray Me - one who is eating with Me." They were saddened, and one by one they said to Him, "Surely you don't mean me?" "It is one of the Twelve," He replied, "one who dips bread into the bowl with Me. The Son of Man will go just as it is written about him. But woe to that man who .... the Son of Man! It would be better for him if he had not been born." While they were eating, Yeshua took ...., and when He had given thanks, he broke it and gave it to his disciples, saying, "Take it; this is My body." Then He took a ...., and when He had given thanks, He gave it to them, and they all drank from it. "This is My .... of the ...., which is poured out for many," He said to them. "Truly I tell you, I will not drink again from the fruit of the vine until that day when I drink it new in the .... of God.""

"**This is my body, which is given for you. Do this in remembrance of Me.**"

(Luke 22:19)

The upper room

Before Yeshua was crucified, He shared a final meal with His disciples in an upper room in Jerusalem. Read John 13:1-38, which describes betrayal, a new commandment, and Peter's denial. Then select one of these topics and imagine what the disciples might have said to one another when they heard these things. Fill in the speech bubbles to show their conversation. Then, color the picture and answer the question below.

During the last supper, what did Yeshua teach you about being a servant?

....
....
....
....

Yeshua shared His final meal with the twelve disciples He had chosen to be His closest followers (Luke 6:13-16; John 13). Unscramble the words to learn the names of the twelve disciples who were with Him at the Last Supper.

tPree ....

nAedwr ....

seaJm ....

hJon ....

ipPihl ....

omlwrtBahoe ....

etwtaMh ....

soThma ....

aseJm (osn fo paeAuhls) ....

dJeu ....

oSnmi ....

uasJd ocalitsr ....

✷ Read about The Last Supper in Matthew 26, Mark 14, Luke 22, and John 13.

Yeshua and the Twelve

Read Matthew 4 and 11, Mark 1 and 3, Luke 5-6, 9-10, and 14, John 13, and the article below to learn how Yeshua called His disciples, what it meant to follow Him, and the commitment required to be a disciple.

How did young Hebrew men become disciples, and what did it require? In ancient Israel, discipleship was a structured way of learning from a teacher of the Torah. Before becoming a disciple, a young man first learned the Scriptures in a community setting. This early instruction prepared him to understand Yah's laws and statues.

After receiving this basic instruction, a young man who wished to continue learning might seek out a respected teacher and ask to become his disciple. The teacher carefully evaluated the student to see if he showed ability, discipline, and commitment. Not every student was accepted. If the teacher believed the student was ready, he invited him with words such as "Follow me." This invitation carried great meaning, since only a small number of students were chosen for discipleship.

Once accepted, a disciple left his normal routine behind. Many disciples left their homes, jobs, and sometimes their families to travel with their teacher for long periods of time. They followed closely, learning not only through lessons, but by watching how the teacher lived each day. Jewish writings describe this as being covered in the "dust of the rabbi's feet," meaning the disciple followed so closely that he learned through constant observation.

This helps explain how Yeshua gathered His twelve disciples. According to the Bible, Yeshua called men from different walks of life, including fishermen and a tax collector, and invited them with the words, "Come, follow Me." Over time, He chose twelve men to be His closest disciples. They left their work and followed Him, learning directly from His teaching, actions, and example. The goal of discipleship was not only to remember teachings, but to imitate the teacher's entire way of life, including prayer, study of Scripture, observance of the Sabbath, treatment of others, and acts of kindness.

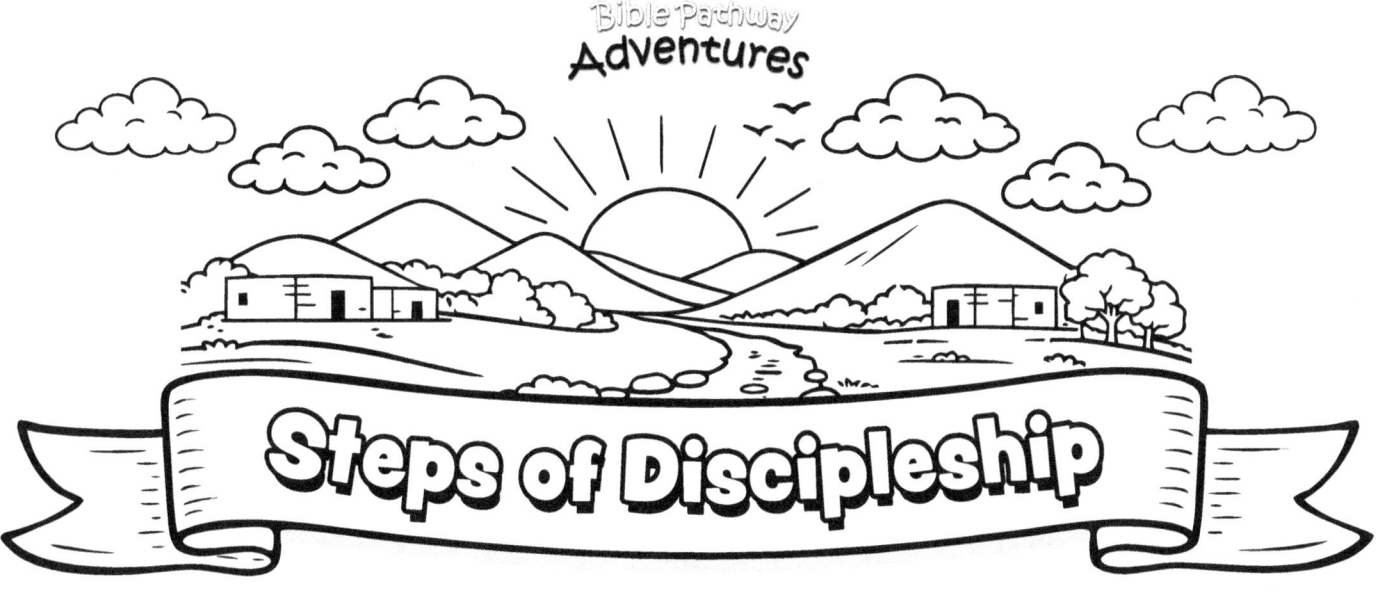

Steps of Discipleship

Read the article, Yeshua and the Twelve.
Then read the events below that describe how a young man became a disciple in ancient Israel. Number the events in the correct order, starting with 1 for what happened first.

	1		
Traveled with his Teacher	Learned the Torah in a community setting	Imitated his teacher's way of life	Asked a teacher to become his disciple

Learned by watching and listening	Received an invitation to "Follow me"	Left home and daily work	Evaluated by the Teacher

Yeshua told His disciples to go and make disciples of all nations (Matthew 28:19). How do you become a disciple of Yeshua today?

....
....
....

A renewed commandment

At the Last Supper in Jerusalem, Yeshua shared with His disciples a *renewed covenant commandment (John 13). This command was based on Deuteronomy 6:4-5, which tells the people of Israel to love Yah with all their heart, soul, and strength, and Leviticus 19:18, which says, "Love your neighbor as yourself." What did Yeshua say? Each number represents a letter of the alphabet. Substitute each number with the correct letter to reveal the answer.

A	B	C	D	E	F	G	H	I	J	K	L	M
1	2	3	4	5	6	7	8	9	10	11	12	13
N	O	P	Q	R	S	T	U	V	W	X	Y	Z
14	15	16	17	18	19	20	21	22	23	24	25	26

1. 12 – 15 – 22 – 5: _____
2. 15 – 14 – 5: _____
3. 1 – 14 – 15 – 20 – 8 – 5 – 18: _____
4. 1 – 19: _____
5. 9: _____
6. 8 – 1 – 22 – 5: _____
7. 12 – 15 – 22 – 5 – 4: _____
8. 25 – 15 – 21: _____

*Some Bible translations, such as the ISR, use the word "renewed" commandment. Others, such as the ESV, use the word "new."

Final instructions

During the Last Supper, Yeshua taught His disciples, prepared them for what was about to happen, and gave them instructions about love, servanthood, and the gift of the Holy Spirit (John 13-17). Discuss what Yeshua taught that night and how you can apply His teachings to your everyday life. Then complete the worksheet below.

| 1 = Brown | 2 = Tan | 3 = Red | 4 = Grey |

Read John 14:15. How did Yeshua say you are to love Him?

Why do you think Judas wanted to betray Yeshua?

List five key topics that Yeshua taught His disciples during the meal?

Write a story

Imagine you are a disciple at the Last Supper. Read Matthew 26:1-56 and Luke 22:1-53. Write a short paragraph describing your final meal with Yeshua in Jerusalem. Be sure to include details like the food you ate, who was there, the discussions you had, and what happened after the meal.

....
....
....
....
....
....
....
....
....

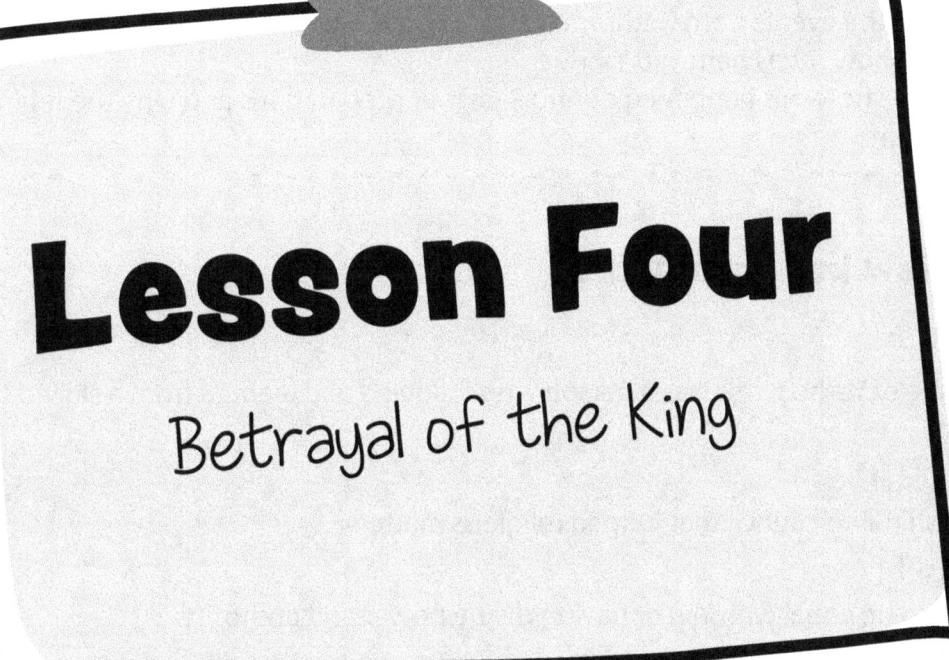

Lesson Four
Betrayal of the King

Betrayal of the King

Matthew 26, Mark 14, Luke 22, and John 18

1. Lesson objectives:

During this lesson, students will:
* Identify the events from Gethsemane to Yeshua's trial before the Sanhedrin.
* Explain how Judas betrayed Yeshua.
* Describe how this happened during Passover preparations and why the timing was important.

2. Review key vocabulary:

◎ **DISCIPLE:**
At the time of Yeshua, this was a person who followed and learned from a skilled teacher of the Torah.

◎ **SANHEDRIN:**
The Jewish ruling council that judged religious matters.

◎ **BLASPHEMY:**
Claiming to be equal with Yah or having divine power and authority.

◎ **BETRAY:**
To turn against or harm someone who trusts you.

◎ **GETHSEMANE:**
A garden of olive trees on the Mount of Olives.

3. Bible memory verse:

"My Father, if it be possible, let this cup pass from Me; nevertheless, not as I will, but as You will." (Matthew 26:39)

Object lesson idea

Show an olive branch or a picture of an olive tree. Explain that just as olives are pressed to make oil, Yeshua faced great pressure in the Garden of Gethsemane, yet He chose to obey Yah.

Did you know?

The Garden of Gethsemane was located on the Mount of Olives. Olive presses were common in this area, and the name 'Gethsemane' means "oil press."

 **4. Read Matthew 26, Mark 14, Luke 22, John 18, or read the Bible story below:**

After Yeshua and His disciples had shared a meal together, they left Jerusalem and walked through the Kidron Valley to the Garden of Gethsemane. Behind them, the city was still full of activity. Families were preparing their homes, and priests were getting ready to sacrifice the Passover lambs at the Temple. In the garden, Yeshua asked His disciples to pray. Then He went a short distance away and prayed in deep sorrow, knowing what was about to happen. Three times He asked if there was another way, yet each time He chose to obey Yah's will. While He was still speaking, Judas arrived. Having already planned with the chief priests, he came with soldiers carrying swords and clubs. Judas greeted Yeshua with a kiss, the agreed sign to show them whom to arrest. The soldiers seized Yeshua, and the disciples fled in fear. Yeshua was taken first to Annas and then to Caiaphas, the high priest, where members of the Sanhedrin had gathered. The Sanhedrin was the highest Jewish ruling council, made up of chief priests, elders, and teachers of the law. They searched for charges against Him and brought forward false witnesses. When Yeshua declared that He was the Son of Man, they accused Him of blasphemy. Since the religious leaders were not permitted to carry out executions, they took Yeshua to Pontius Pilate, the Roman governor.

 **5. Let's discuss:**

1. Why did Yeshua and His disciples go to the Garden of Gethsemane?
2. What did Yeshua pray about while He was in the garden?
3. How did Judas betray Yeshua?
4. How did the disciples react when Yeshua was arrested?
5. Why did the religious leaders want to arrest Yeshua?
6. Who was the high priest?
7. How did the Sanhedrin decide that Yeshua was guilty?
8. Why was Yeshua sent to Pilate?

 6. Activities:

* Worksheet: Yah's Appointed Times
* Worksheet: Sabbath to Sukkot
* Bible story worksheet: Betrayal of the king
* Worksheet: 30 pieces of silver
* Did you know? worksheet: Judas' betrayal
* Worksheet: Freedom from Roman rule
* Bible quiz: Garden of Gethsemane
* Worksheet: Betrayal in the garden
* Worksheet: Watch and pray
* Worksheet: Yeshua on trial
* Worksheet: Before the Sanhedrin
* Worksheet: Caiaphas, the high priest
* Story sequencing activity: Sequence the story
* Math worksheet: Unleavened math challenge
* Let's learn Hebrew: Feast of Unleavened Bread
* Worksheet: Preparation Day in Jerusalem
* Worksheet: Preparation Day chart

Yah's Appointed Times

Every 7th day
The Sabbath (Shabbat)

14th day of the 1st month
First day of Unleavened Bread
(Passover meal)
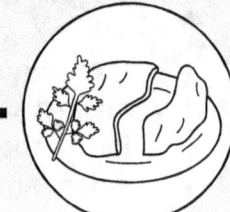

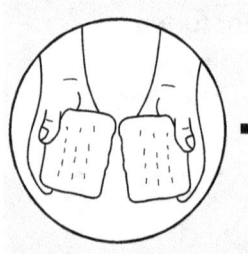
15th- 21st days of the 1st month
Feast of Unleavened Bread (Chag HaMatzot)

50 days after Firstfruits
Feast of Weeks (Shavuot / Pentecost)
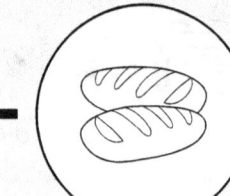

1st day of the 7th month
Feast of Trumpets (Yom Teru'ah)

10th day of the 7th month
Day of Atonement (Yom Kippur)

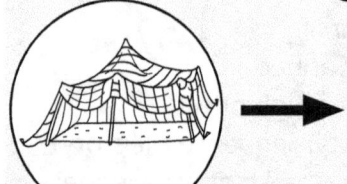
15th- 21st days of the 7th month
Feast of Tabernacles (Sukkot)

22nd day of the 7th month
The Last Great Day (Shemini Atzeret)

Sabbath to Sukkot

Yah gave us special days called Appointed Times, or Feasts, which are listed in Leviticus 23. These are set-apart times to worship Him and learn about His plan to restore the House of Israel. Along with the weekly Sabbath, Passover and the Feast of Unleavened Bread in the spring remind us how Yah delivered His people from Egypt and how Yeshua became our Passover Lamb. The Spring Feasts were fulfilled at Yeshua's first coming, while the Fall Feasts point to His return as King.

 Step 1:

Read Leviticus 23, and write the name and date of each Appointed Time on the timeline.

 **Step 2:**

Use one color to highlight the Spring Feasts and a different color for the Fall Feasts.

 Step 3:

Near the Feast of Unleavened Bread banner, write one fact from Leviticus 23 about this Appointed Time.

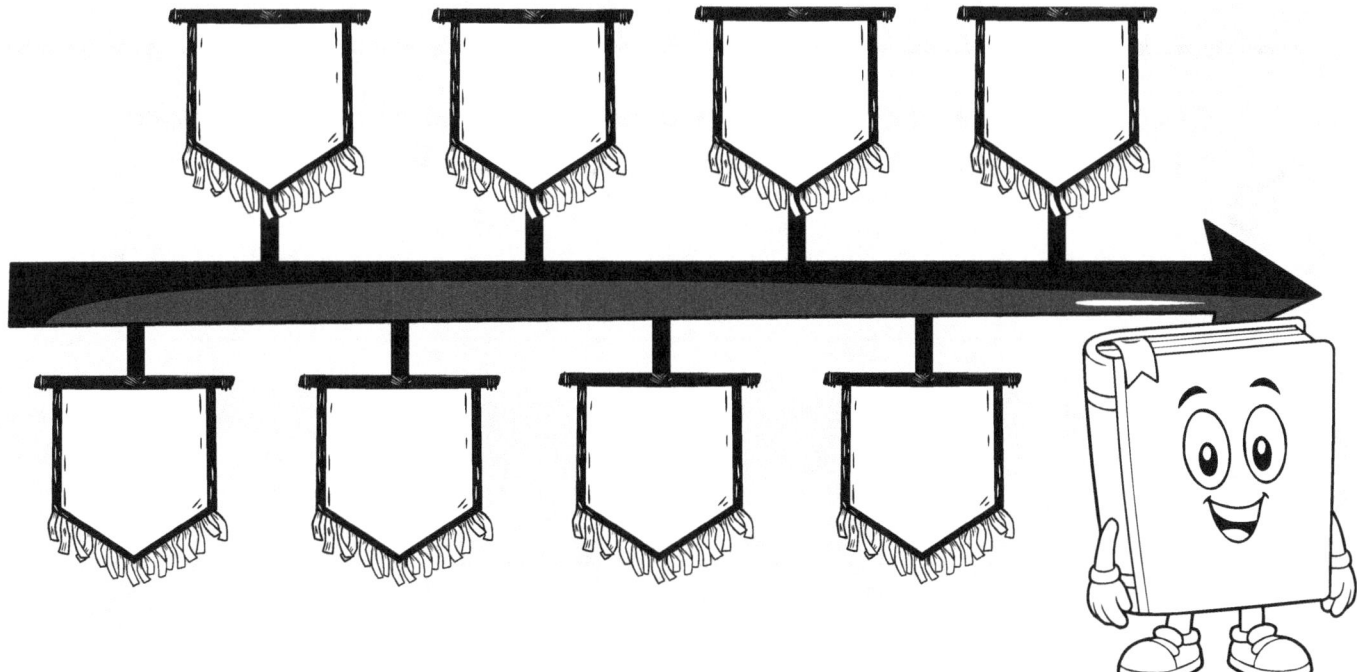

Betrayal of the King

Yeshua gathered with His disciples for a final meal in Jerusalem, but one of them would betray Him. Read John 13:1-30 and the Bible story below, then answer the question.

Yeshua and His disciples met in a house in Jerusalem to share a final meal. Reclining on cushions, Yeshua said, "I have wanted to eat this meal with you before I die. But I will not eat it again until we eat together in the Kingdom of God." He then took a cup of wine, gave thanks, and passed it around the room. "Take this and drink it," He said. Then He took some bread, blessed it, and broke it into pieces. "From now on, do this to remember Me. This bread represents My body, which is being broken for you."

As the disciples ate, Yeshua stood up from the table. He poured water into a basin and began to wash His disciples' feet. Peter said, "No, Master! You will never wash my feet. That is a servant's job!" Yeshua replied, "If you do not let Me wash your feet, you cannot be My disciple. I am giving you an example to follow." After washing their feet, Yeshua said, "Tonight, one of you will betray Me." The disciples stopped eating and looked at one another. "Master, who would do such a thing?" they asked. "Is it him? Is it me?"

"It is the one to whom I give this bread," Yeshua said quietly. He took a piece of bread, dipped it in olive oil, and handed it to Judas. "Do what you must do." Ha'Satan had already put it into Judas's heart to betray Yeshua. He left the room and stepped into the night. It was time to betray the King…

Why do you think Yeshua shared a meal with Judas, even though He knew that Judas would betray Him?

30 pieces of silver

Tyrian shekels were coins of Tyre, and were the only currency accepted at the Jerusalem temple. It is widely accepted by Bible scholars that the religious leaders paid Judas shekels of Tyre (30 pieces of silver) to betray the Messiah. The silver shekels and half-shekels of Tyre were minted from c. 126 B.C. until c. 57 A.D. Read Matthew 26 and Luke 22 and then answer the questions.

① Why did Judas agree to betray Yeshua for just 30 pieces of silver?

....
....
....

② When Yeshua said one of His disciples would betray Him, why do you think Judas still asked, "Is it me?" even though he had already made the deal to turn Yeshua in?

....
....
....

Design your own silver shekel

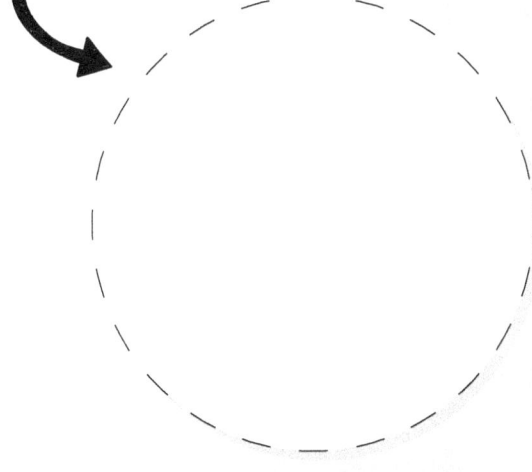

③ How did Judas show the soldiers which person was Yeshua in the garden of Gethsemane?

....
....
....

Did You Know?

Some Bible scholars believe Judas was part of a group called the Zealots, who wanted to free Israel from Roman rule. Judas may have been disappointed that Yeshua did not defeat the Romans or become king. He might have thought that by arranging Yeshua's arrest, he could force Him to show His power as Israel's Messiah. But Judas did not understand the Scriptures that said Yeshua would first come as a suffering servant (Isaiah 53).

Draw Judas meeting with the chief priests to betray Yeshua.

Freedom from Roman rule

At the time of Yeshua, the land of Judea was under Roman rule. Many Israelites were angry about Roman cruelty, heavy taxes, and unfair governors, and they longed for freedom from this control. One group that strongly opposed Roman rule was the Zealots. They were patriots who believed force could be used to remove the Romans. The Zealots followed the Torah closely and believed that Roman taxes and laws went against Yah's commands. Read the paragraphs below. Then write in the chart the type of freedom the Zealots were seeking and compare it to the type of freedom Yah offers when we follow His commands.

The Zealot movement began around AD 6, when a man named Judas of Galilee led a revolt against a Roman census used to collect taxes. He taught that only Yah should rule Israel, not a foreign emperor like Caesar. His ideas spread, and the Zealots became more active. Some lived in hiding and attacked Roman soldiers. A more extreme group, called the Sicarii, carried small daggers and secretly killed their enemies in crowded places.

The Zealots urged Israelites to rebel and hoped for a Messiah who would lead them to victory over Rome. Three of Yeshua's disciples, Simon the Zealot, Simon Peter, and Judas Iscariot, may have been connected to this movement. Yeshua and His disciples were in Jerusalem for the Feast of Unleavened Bread when Judas betrayed Him to the religious leaders. Judas may have believed that if Yeshua were the true Savior of Israel, He would fight back and begin a revolt against Rome. Instead, Yeshua did not resist arrest.

Freedom the Zealots Wanted	Freedom Yah Provides

Garden of GETHSEMANE

Read Matthew 26:1-56, Luke 22:1-53, and John 13:1-18:24. Answer the questions below.

1. Where did Yeshua eat a meal with His disciples before His arrest?

2. In which garden did Yeshua pray before He was arrested by the religious leaders?

3. While Yeshua was praying, what happened to Peter, James, and John?

4. Which disciple did Yeshua warn would deny Him three times?

5. How did Judas betray Yeshua in the garden?

6. Who appeared to Yeshua in the garden to give Him strength?

7. What did the religious leaders give Judas in exchange for betraying Yeshua?

8. Which Appointed Time (Feast) had Yeshua come to Jerusalem to observe?

9. What happened to the disciples after Yeshua was arrested?

10. After the temple guards arrested Yeshua, where did they take Him?

Betrayal in the garden

Judas, one of Yeshua's disciples, betrayed Him in the Garden of Gethsemane by leading a group of soldiers and religious leaders to arrest Him. To show them who Yeshua was, Judas gave Him a kiss, a sign of friendship that he used for betrayal. Read each statement about what happened, then decide if it is true or false by checking the correct box. Use what you know from Matthew 26, John 18, and Luke 22 to help you answer.

True or False?

1. Yeshua prayed three times before He was arrested. ◯ True ◯ False
2. The disciples stayed awake and prayed with Yeshua. ◯ True ◯ False
3. Judas identified Yeshua to the soldiers by shaking His hand. ◯ True ◯ False
4. Yeshua told Peter to put away his sword after he cut off the servant's ear. ◯ True ◯ False
5. An angel came to strengthen Yeshua. ◯ True ◯ False
6. Yeshua tried to escape but was caught by the high priest. ◯ True ◯ False

Watch and pray

Yeshua went to the Garden of Gethsemane to pray to His Father. He was troubled and asked His disciples to stay awake and pray so that they would not enter into temptation. Read Matthew 26:36-46 and complete the chart to show Yeshua's actions and how they compared with those of His disciples.

Yeshua's actions	The disciples' actions
....	....
....	....
....	....
....	....
....	....
....	....
....	....
....	....
....	....

Why do you think it was difficult for Peter, James, and John to stay awake?

....

....

....

Yeshua on trial

A meeting of the Sanhedrin was a serious and formal event. This Jewish ruling council had seventy-one members, including the High Priest, former high priests, elders, scribes, and leaders from the Pharisees and Sadducees. They met in a hall called the Chamber of Hewn Stone, located on the Temple Mount in Jerusalem. During meetings, the members sat in a wide semi-circle so they could see and hear one another. The High Priest led from the center while witnesses stood before them. The Sanhedrin asked questions, debated during the day, and made decisions by a vote.

Yeshua's trial, however, broke all these rules. Late at night, around the 14th of Nisan, the Day of Preparation for Passover, the leaders met secretly in the home of the High Priest, Caiaphas, instead of in the Chamber of Hewn Stone. Holding a trial at night was against the law, yet false witnesses were quickly brought in. When their stories did not agree, Caiaphas asked Yeshua, "Are You the Messiah, the Son of God?" When Yeshua replied that He was, the council decided He should be put to death. But because they did not have the authority to carry out a death sentence under Roman rule, they sent Him early the next morning to Pontius Pilate, the Roman governor (Mark 15:1).

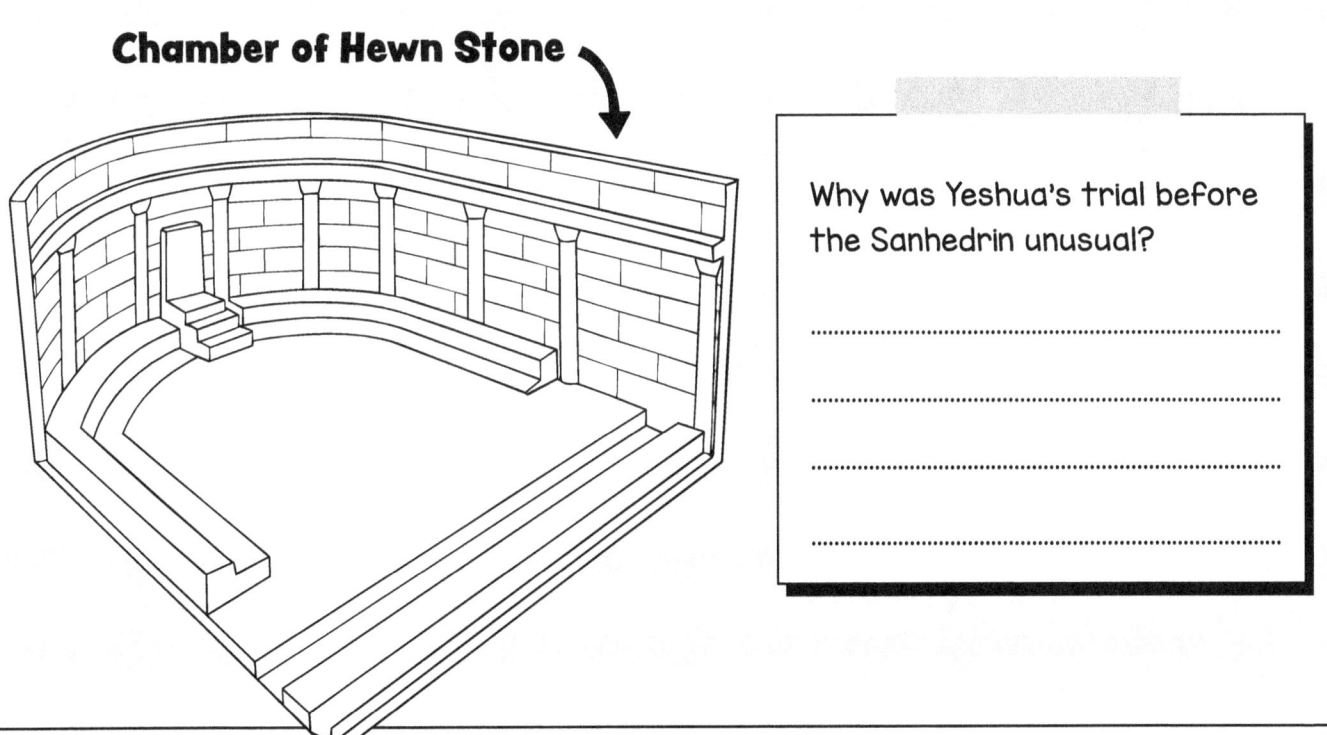

Chamber of Hewn Stone

Why was Yeshua's trial before the Sanhedrin unusual?

Before the Sanhedrin

Read Matthew 26, Mark 14, and Luke 22 to learn what happened when Yeshua was taken before the Sanhedrin, the Jewish ruling council. The Sanhedrin was made up of priests, elders, and teachers of the Torah who met to make important religious and legal decisions. The Bible mentions some of the people who were present that night. Write the name or title of each person or group below their portrait, then answer the questions.

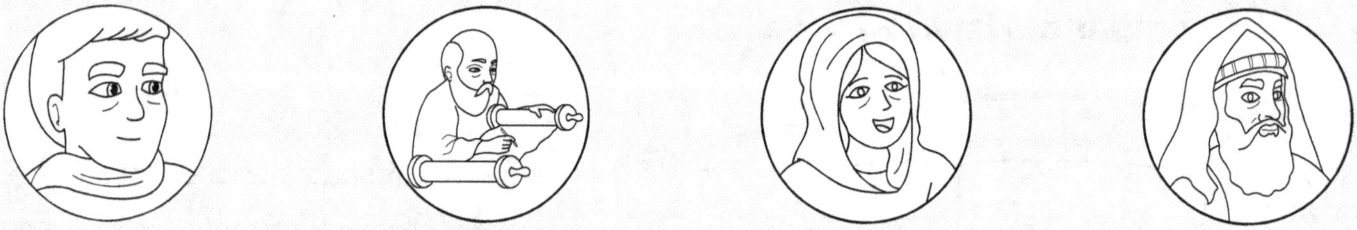

Discussion questions:

1. What false witnesses came forward, and what did they accuse Yeshua of saying?

2. What did Peter do while Yeshua was on trial?

3. What decision did the Sanhedrin make about Yeshua?

Caiaphas, the high priest, owned a large mansion on Jerusalem's western hill. Archaeologists have found remains of courtyards, mikvahs, and rooms for servants. Read Mark 14 and John 18 and then answer the questions below.

① After the Temple guards arrested Yeshua, where did they take Him first?

....

② Who was the religious leader, Annas?

....

③ What question did Caiaphas ask Yeshua?

....

Sequence the story

Read Matthew 26, Mark 14, Luke 22, and John 18, and review the ten sentences below. They recount the story of Yeshua's last supper and trial, but the events are out of order. Your task is to arrange them correctly.
Write a number next to each sentence to show the proper sequence of events.

A. .... Judas arrived with soldiers and temple guards, greeted Yeshua with a kiss, and they arrested Him.

B. .... During the meal, Yeshua took bread, gave thanks, broke it, and said, "This is My body given for you."

C. .... The disciples fled, but Peter followed at a distance to the courtyard of the high priest's palace, where he denied knowing Yeshua three times.

D. .... After singing from the Psalms, Yeshua led the disciples across the Kidron Valley to the Garden of Gethsemane.

E. .... That night, the Sanhedrin met in the palace of the High Priest, Caiaphas, and accused Yeshua of blasphemy.

F. .... In the garden, Yeshua prayed in deep sorrow while Peter, James, and John fell asleep nearby.

G. .... At sunrise, the council tied Yeshua up and sent Him to Pontius Pilate, the Roman governor, for judgment.

H. .... Yeshua told His disciples that one of them would betray Him, and Judas left the room and went into the night.

I. .... He lifted a cup of wine and said, "This cup that is poured out for you is the renewed* covenant in my blood."

J. .... Yeshua and His twelve disciples gathered in an upper room in Jerusalem to share a final meal.

Unleavened Math Challenge!

(Based on Deuteronomy 16:3-4)

Directions: Solve each math problem below. Show your work in the boxes.

Removing the Leaven

Each Israelite home had three rooms that needed to be cleaned of leaven. If it took 15 minutes to search each room, how many minutes did it take to clean the whole house?

Baking for the Feast

An Israelite woman baked unleavened bread (matzah) for her family before the Feast began. She used 3 cups of flour for each batch, and each batch made 12 loaves of unleavened bread. If she baked 4 batches to feed her family for all seven days, how many loaves did she bake in total?

Feeding the Pilgrims

During Yeshua's time, about 400,000 pilgrims traveled to Jerusalem for the Feast of Unleavened Bread. If each pilgrim ate two pieces of unleavened bread per day for seven days, how much bread was eaten during the entire Feast?

Chag HaMatzot

The Hebrew name for the Feast of Unleavened Bread is Chag HaMatzot. This feast honors the journey of the children of Israel out of the land of Egypt, when Yah asked the Israelites to eat unleavened bread (bread without yeast) for seven days. Yeshua was in Jerusalem during this Feast to honor Yah's Appointed Time with His disciples. He fulfilled this Feast by being crucified at the same time the Passover lambs were being slaughtered at the Temple in Jerusalem. He rose from the grave during on Firstfruits, during the week of Unleavened Bread.

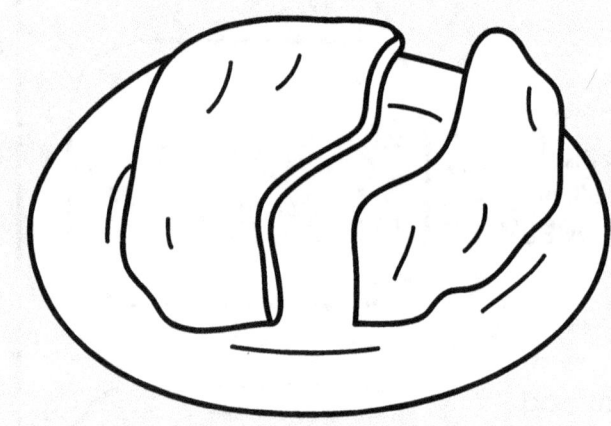

Feast of

Unleavened Bread

Trace the Hebrew name here:	Write the Hebrew name here:
חג המצות	
חג המצות	

Let's write!

Practice writing 'Chag HaMatzot' on the lines below.

חג המצות

חג המצות

Try this on your own.
Remember that Hebrew is read from RIGHT to LEFT.

_____

_____

How did Yeshua fulfill the Feast of Unleavened Bread?

....
....
....
....

Bible Pathway Adventures

Preparation Day in Jerusalem

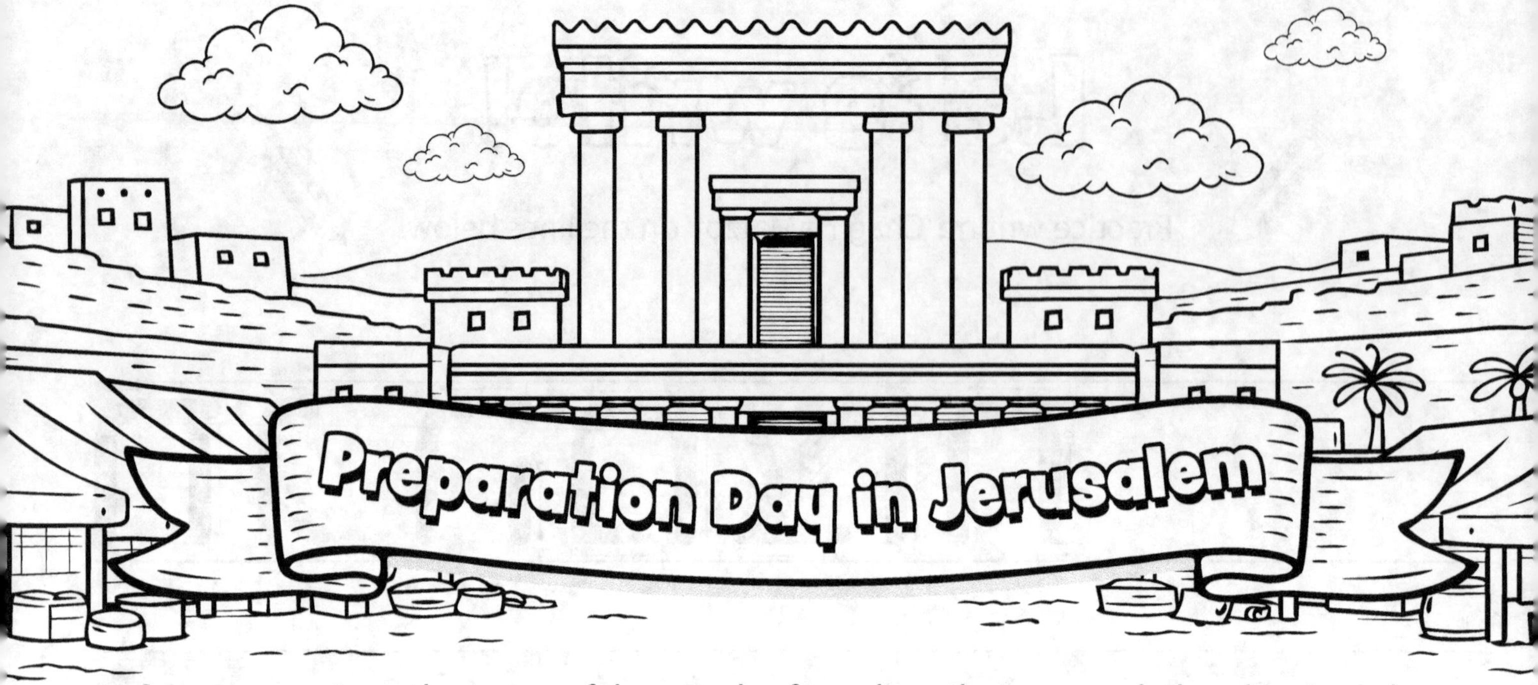

In first-century Jerusalem, tens of thousands of Israelite pilgrims traveled to the city to keep the Feast of Unleavened Bread. Families brought their lambs to the Temple, where the priests sacrificed them. Afterward, they took the lambs home to roast and prepare for the meal. The city was filled with excitement as everyone got ready to remember how God rescued the children of Israel from the land of Egypt.

Matthew 27:1-50, Mark 15:1-39, Luke 23:1-46, and John 18:28-19:30 tell what happened on Preparation Day in Jerusalem. Imagine you are an ancient Israelite. Create a checklist of tasks a family in first century Jerusalem would complete on Preparation Day, based on the timeline chart on the next page.

Preparation Day checklist

- [ ] ....
- [ ] ....
- [ ] ....
- [ ] ....
- [ ] ....
- [ ] ....
- [ ] ....
- [ ] ....
- [ ] ....
- [ ] ....
- [ ] ....
- [ ] ....

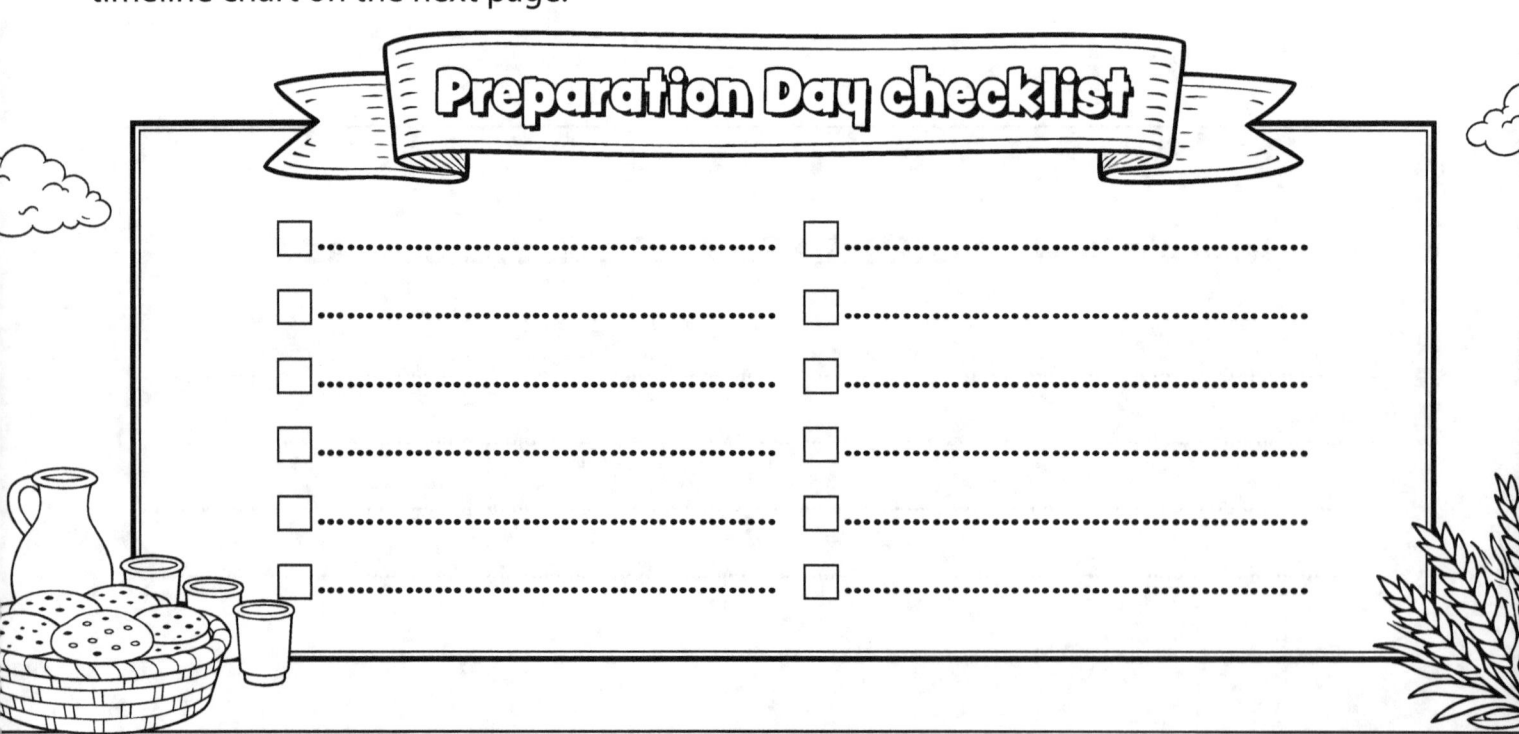

Preparation Day
(Nisan 14)

Time	Event	Preparation day tasks
Mid-Morning (9:00 – 11:00 AM)	Temple Preparations Begin	The priests prepare the temple altar for the Passover lambs to be sacrificed in the afternoon.
Early Afternoon (1:00 – 3:00 PM)	Passover Lambs Sacrificed	Lambs are slaughtered at the Temple (Exodus 12:6). Blood is applied to the altar as families prepare to take their lambs home.
Late Afternoon (3:00 – 5:00 PM)	Lambs Taken Home, Roasting Begins	Each household roasts their lamb over fire as instructed (Exodus 12:8-9).
Before Sunset (5:00 – 6:00 PM) sign	Preparation for the Meal	Families finalize their preparations. The meal must be eaten in haste, with belts fastened, sandals on, and staffs in hand (Exodus 12:11).
Sunset (6:00 – 7:00 PM)	Passover Begins (Nisan 15)	Hebrews eat the Passover meal according to God's command, remembering His deliverance from Egypt (Exodus 12:14).

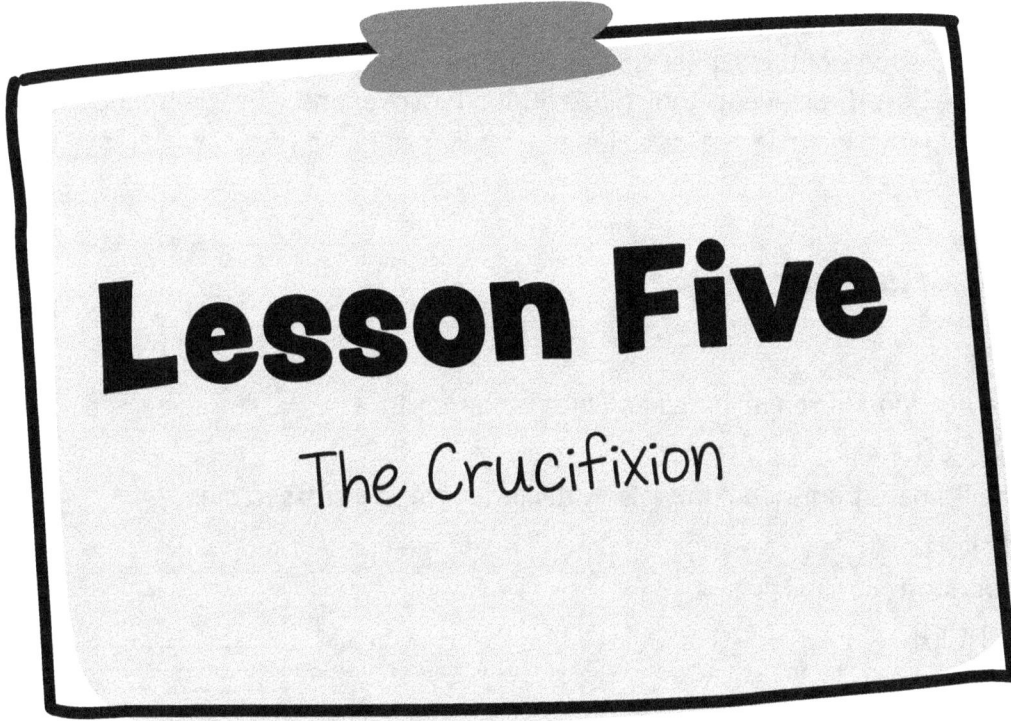

Lesson Five

The Crucifixion

Lesson Plan for: The Crucifixion

Matthew 27, Mark 15, Luke 23, and John 18-19

1. Lesson objectives:

During this lesson, students will:
* Identify the key events from Yeshua's trial before Pilate to His burial.
* Explain the roles of the Sanhedrin and Pilate in Yeshua's death.
* Describe how these events took place during Passover and why the timing mattered.

2. Review key vocabulary:

- **GOLGOTHA:** The place outside Jerusalem; it means 'Place of the Skull'.
- **CRUCIFIXION:** A way the Romans punished criminals by nailing them to a cross to die.
- **SIXTH HOUR:** Midday or noon (12 p.m.).
- **NINTH HOUR:** 3 p.m.
- **EARTHQUAKE:** The ground shakes when the earth's plates move deep underground.

3. Bible memory verse:

"They crucified Yeshua and divided His garments among them, casting lots for them, to decide what each should take." (Mark 15:24)

Did you know?

Yeshua died on the cross at the same time the Passover lambs were being sacrificed at the Temple in Jerusalem for the Passover meal.

Object lesson idea

Turn off the lights or dim the room for a short moment and ask students to sit quietly. Explain that while Yeshua was on the cross, darkness covered the land for three hours, something that did not normally happen during the day.

4. Read Matthew 27, Mark 15, Luke 23, and John 18-19, or read the Bible story below:

After Yeshua appeared before the Sanhedrin, He was taken to Pilate, the Roman governor, because the religious leaders did not have authority to put Him to death. Pilate questioned Him and found no crime worthy of death. Still, the crowd demanded crucifixion and asked for Barabbas to be released. Wanting to satisfy the crowd, Pilate handed Yeshua over to be executed. The Roman soldiers led Him away, whipped Him, and placed a crown of thorns on His head. They ordered Him to carry His crossbeam to Golgotha. When He became too weak to continue, they forced Simon of Cyrene to carry it. At Golgotha they offered Him a bitter drink, but He refused. They nailed Him to the stake and raised it up. A sign above Him read, "King of the Jews." Many people mocked Him, including the religious leaders. From the sixth hour, darkness covered the land for three hours. It was Preparation Day, and families were preparing for Passover while lambs were being sacrificed at the Temple. At the ninth hour, Yeshua cried out and gave up His spirit. At that moment the Temple veil was torn in two, the earth shook, and tombs were opened. Many saints were raised and later appeared in the city. A Roman centurion said, "Truly, this was the Son of God!" Because the Sabbath was near, Joseph of Arimathea asked Pilate for Yeshua's body. He wrapped it in linen cloth and placed it in a new tomb cut from rock.

5. Let's discuss:

1. Why did the religious leaders bring Yeshua to Pilate instead of killing Him themselves?
2. What questions did Pilate ask Yeshua during the trial?
3. Why do you think Pilate chose to release Barabbas instead of Yeshua?
4. What happened to Yeshua after Pilate gave his decision?
5. What signs or events took place while Yeshua was on the cross?
6. How did the Roman centurion respond after Yeshua died?
7. Why was Yeshua buried before sunset on Preparation Day?
8. Who placed Yeshua in the tomb?

6. Activities:

- Coloring worksheet: Yeshua before Pilate
- Bible crossword puzzle: Pontius Pilate
- Coloring page: Walking to Golgotha
- Worksheet: Journey to Golgotha
- Newspaper worksheet: The Jerusalem Times
- Coloring worksheet: Your Passover meal
- Worksheet: The Passover Lamb
- Bible quiz: The Crucifixion
- Creative writing: The Crucifixion
- Worksheet: Betrayal and the cross
- Worksheet: The Passover meal
- Worksheet: Into the tomb
- Coloring page: Into the tomb
- Worksheet: Passover in Jerusalem
- Bible quiz: Feast of Unleavened Bread
- Coloring worksheet: The centurion's statement
- Bible craft: Make a Passover banner

Yeshua before Pilate

A Roman praetorium was the official home and workplace of a Roman governor. It was where trials were held and important decisions were made. On Preparation Day, just before the Feast of Unleavened Bread, Yeshua was brought to the praetorium in Jerusalem to stand before Pilate. Read the Bible story in Matthew 27, Mark 15, Luke 23, and John 18-19. Then complete the chart below to show the order of events and color the picture of a praetorium.

Stage	Event	What happened?
1	The chief priests' accusations.	....
2	What Pilate learned about Yeshua.	....
3	The crowd's demands.	....
4	Pilate's decision.	....

Pontius PILATE

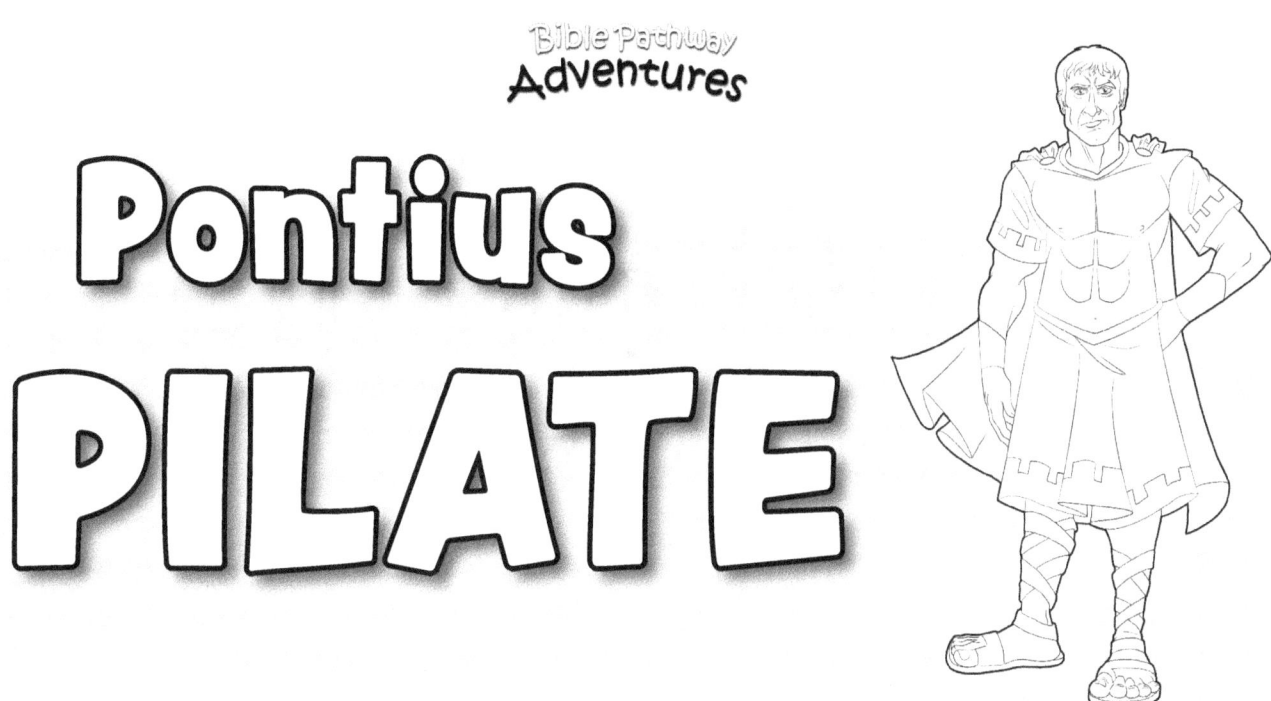

Read Matthew 27 and John 18. Complete the crossword below.

ACROSS

3) Yeshua said His kingdom is not of this _____.
6) The place where Yeshua was crucified.
7) The Roman governor who questioned Yeshua.
8) The Roman soldiers placed a crown of _____ on Yeshua's head.
10) The crowd shouted for Yeshua to be _____.

DOWN

1) Pilate sat on the _____ seat when he judged Yeshua.
2) Yeshua was taken inside the governor's headquarters, called the _____.
4) Who asked Pilate for Yeshua's body?
5) The man released instead of Yeshua.
9) The sign placed above Yeshua on the stake said "King of the _____."

Journey to Golgotha

Pontius Pilate sentenced Yeshua to die by crucifixion. Why did this happen? Read Mark 15:1-32, then draw or write a short summary of Yeshua's journey to Golgotha.

Answer the questions below.

Who sentenced Yeshua to die on the cross?

Who helped carry Yeshua's crossbeam to Golgotha?

What did the soldiers write on a sign above Yeshua's head?

City of Jerusalem

The Jerusalem Times

LAND OF ISRAEL — A PASSOVER PUBLICATION

Barabbas freed!

....

....

....

....

....

....

Pilate sentences Messiah

....

....

....

....

City lamb shortage

Your Passover meal

1) What is unleavened bread (matzah), and why do you eat it?
....
....
....
....

2) What are bitter herbs, and why do you eat them?
....
....
....
....

3) What does the cup of liquid remind you of, and why do you drink it?
....
....
....
....

4) Where is the Lamb?
....
....

The Passover lamb

When Israel had a Temple, in addition to the unblemished lamb for each family, a lamb was chosen by the high priest to die for the sin of the nation. Four days before the Passover (10th Nisan), this lamb was led in a huge procession from Bethany to the Temple. During the procession, the people waved palm branches and sang Psalms. Did you know that Yeshua rode into Jerusalem to the Temple on the very same day as the procession of the lamb chosen to die for the sin of the nation? By doing this, He became "the Lamb of Yah who takes away the sin of the world" (John 1:29), fulfilling ancient prophecies of the coming Messiah.

Just as the Passover lamb was examined for four days before the Feast, the religious leaders questioned Yeshua in the Temple for four days before Passover. On the morning of the Day of Preparation, the eve of Passover, Yeshua was beaten and prepared for death, just as the lambs were prepared for sacrifice in the Temple (Matthew 27:26). The prophet Isaiah wrote, "He was wounded for our transgressions, He was bruised for our iniquities" (Isaiah 53:5). Yeshua died at the same time the unblemished lambs were slain, at the ninth hour or three o'clock in the afternoon. The Bible says the lambs were to be killed "between the evenings" (Exodus 12:6). This phrase refers to the same time the priests called "the ninth hour."

Answer the questions below.

Why did Yeshua ride into Jerusalem on the same day the Passover lambs were chosen?

How did Yeshua's death fulfill this Appointed Time?

Was Yeshua the Passover lamb? Explain your answer.

The CRUCIFIXION

Read Matthew 27:32-56. Answer the questions below.

1. Who sentenced Yeshua to die?

2. Who was forced to carry Yeshua's crossbeam through the streets of Jerusalem?

3. At which place outside Jerusalem was Yeshua nailed to the cross?

4. What was written on the sign above Yeshua's head?

5. What did Yeshua cry out while He was nailed to the cross?

6. Who was crucified next to Yeshua?

7. After Yeshua died, how long did darkness cover the land?

8. What did the Roman soldier use to pierce Yeshua's side?

9. What happened to some of the saints after Yeshua died?

10. Name two of the women who watched Yeshua's crucifixion.

Write a story

Imagine you are an ancient Israelite living in Jerusalem. Describe what you saw and heard on the day that Yeshua was crucified at Golgotha.

....
....
....
....
....
....
....
....
....

Betrayal and the cross

Read Isaiah 53, Matthew 26 and Mark 15. Judas thought he could force Yeshua to reveal Himself as Israel's king by arranging His arrest. But Judas didn't understand that Yeshua's mission was different. He came to suffer and die for our sins, just as the Bible said. Yah's plan was much greater than Judas's plan! In one column, write about how Judas betrayed Yeshua. In the other column, write about Yah's plan.

Judas

Yeshua:

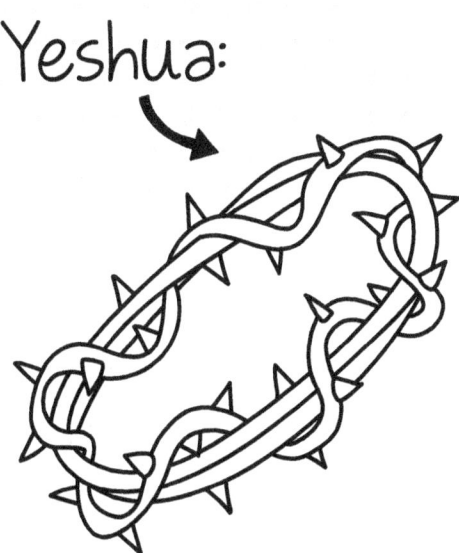

Write about Judas' plan vs Yah's plan.

....	....
....	....
....	....
....	....
....	....

Bible Pathway Adventures

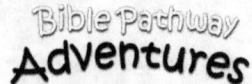

The Passover meal

What do you eat for the Passover meal? Draw the food you eat on the plate below.

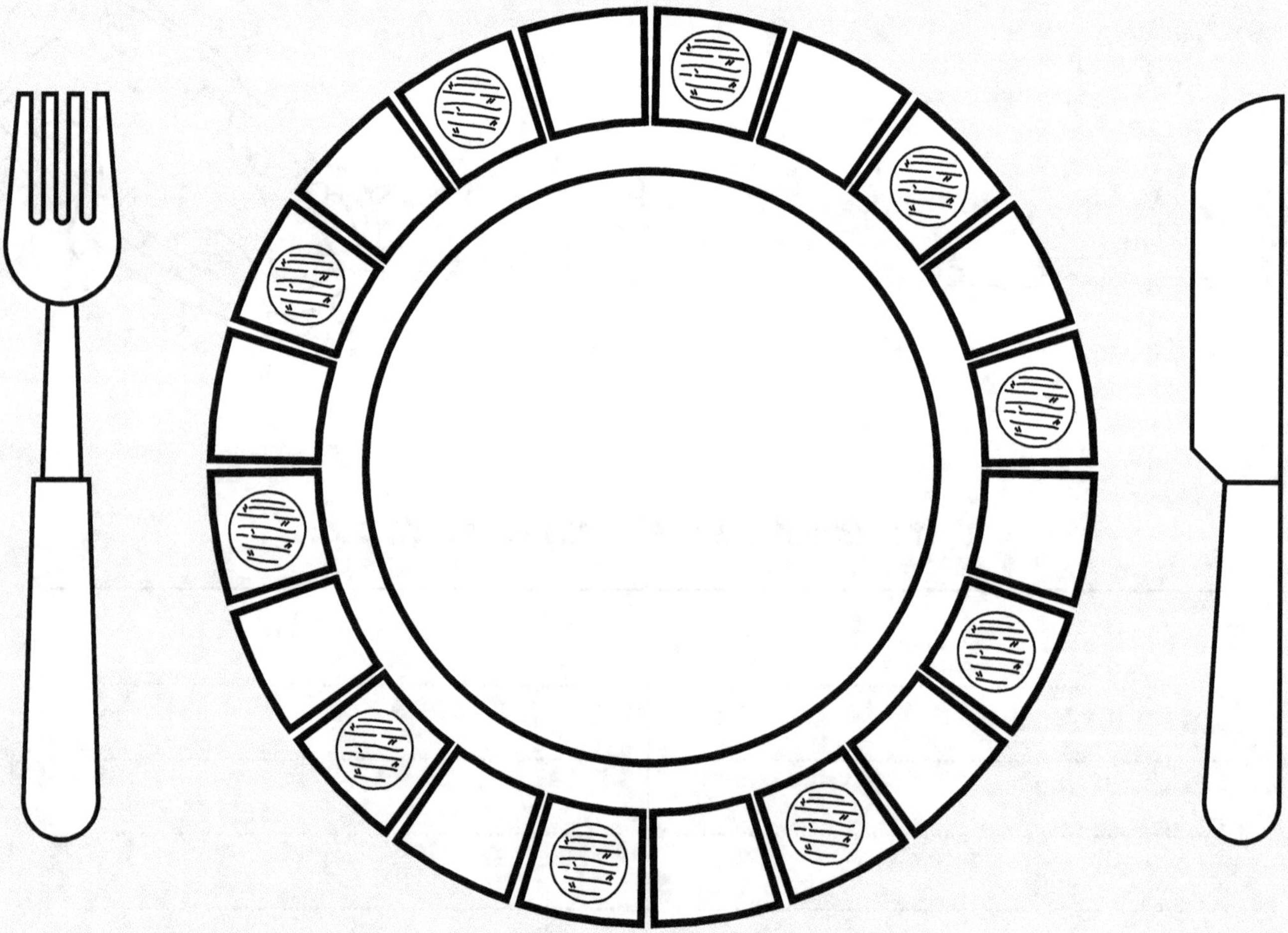

NAME: ....

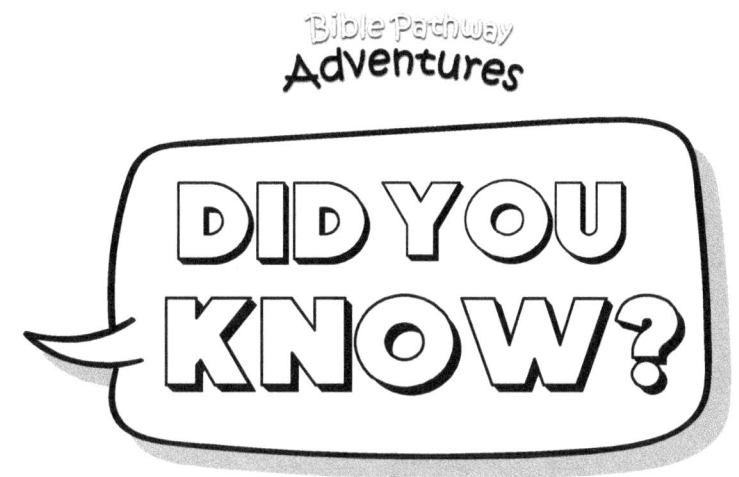

A secret disciple of Yeshua asked to bury Him

Joseph of Arimathea was a secret disciple of Yeshua and a member of the Jewish religious council called the Sanhedrin. He had not agreed with their decision to have Yeshua put to death. Gathering his courage, he went to Pilate, the Roman governor of Judea, and asked for permission to take Yeshua's body (John 19:38). Pilate was surprised to hear that Yeshua had already died. "Is this true?" he asked his soldiers. "Crucified men usually take much longer to die." When Pilate learned that it was true, he ordered the body to be taken down from the cross and given to Joseph.

With the help of his friend Nicodemus, Joseph carefully wrapped the body with a white linen cloth and placed it in his own new tomb cut out of solid rock. Opposite the tomb, the women who had come from Galilee watched to see where Yeshua's body was placed. Then they hurried into the city to prepare spices and perfume for His body. Just before the sun began to set, Joseph and Nicodemus rolled a large stone in front of the tomb so no one could go in or out. At the same time, the sky over Jerusalem filled with smoke from ovens roasting thousands of Passover lambs. People gathered to eat the lamb and to remember how Yah had helped their ancestors escape from slavery in Egypt.

Discuss: why do you think Joseph of Arimathea was a secret disciple of Yeshua?

....

....

....

....

"**Joseph took the body and wrapped it in a linen cloth and laid it in his own new tomb..."**

(Matthew 27:59)

Passover in Jerusalem

During Preparation Day in Jerusalem, the city was busy as families and priests got ready for the Passover meal. In each panel, draw a picture that shows one of the key events from Preparation Day, such as the inspection and slaughter of Passover lambs, altar offerings, and the eating of the Passover meal.

TEMPLE GATES OPEN!

ANIMALS INSPECTED

SACRIFICE OF ANIMALS AND ALTAR OFFERINGS

PILGRIMS CROWD THE TEMPLE!

FAMILIES EAT PASSOVER MEAL

Feast of UNLEAVENED BREAD

Read Exodus 12-13, Leviticus 23, Deuteronomy 16, 1 Corinthians 5, and Acts 20. Answer the questions below.

1. What does the word 'unleavened' mean?

2. How many days does the Feast of Unleavened Bread last?

3. On which day of the month of Nisan does the Feast of Unleavened Bread begin?

4. What did Yah command the Israelites to remove from their homes before the Feast began?

5. Why did the Israelites eat bread without yeast when they left Egypt?

6. What kind of bread did the Israelites eat during the Feast?

7. Where were all Israelite men commanded to travel for this pilgrimage Feast?

8. During Yeshua's time, what large city did people travel to for the Feast of Unleavened Bread?

9. Which Feast did the apostle Paul encourage Israelites to keep in 1 Corinthians 5?

10. After the Feast of Unleavened Bread, where did Paul sail in Acts 20:6?

The centurion's statement

Read Matthew 27, Mark 15, and Luke 23. Color the picture using the key. Then answer the questions below to learn about what the Roman centurion said when Yeshua died.

1 = blue	
2 = brown	
3 = green	
4 = grey	

What did the centurion say when Yeshua died?

What signs helped the centurion believe this?

Explain how Yeshua is our Passover lamb.

Lesson Six

He is Risen!

He is Risen!
Matthew 27:57-28:15 and John 20:1-29

1. Lesson objectives:

During this lesson, students will:
* Explain the key events from Yeshua's burial to the discovery of the empty tomb.
* Summarize what happened on the first day of the week.
* Describe Yeshua's appearance to His disciples and Thomas's response.

2. Review key vocabulary:

- **JOSEPH OF ARIMATHEA:**
  A disciple of Yeshua.
- **TOMB:**
  A cave-like place or stone chamber where dead bodies are placed.
- **BRIBE:**
  Money or a gift given to someone to make them lie or do something wrong.
- **GALILEE:**
  A region in the northern part of the land of Israel.
- **SABBATH:**
  A day of rest, the biblical Sabbath falls on Saturday.

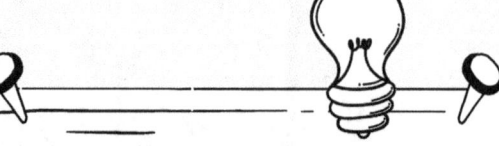

Object lesson idea

Use a small box or jar decorated to look like a tomb. Show students that it is empty and explain that Yeshua's tomb was found empty because He had risen, just as the Bible said would happen.

3. Bible memory verse:

"He is risen! He is not here. See the place where they laid Him." (Mark 16:6)

Did you know?

In the land of Israel, rich men were buried in their own tombs made out of solid rock.

4. Read Matthew 27-28 and John 20, or read the Bible story below:

Joseph and his friend Nicodemus wrapped Yeshua in a clean linen cloth and placed Him in Joseph's new tomb. A large stone was rolled in front of the entrance, while Mary from Magdala and the other Mary watched so they would know where He was laid. They planned to return after the Sabbath to finish preparing His body. The chief priests and Pharisees remembered that Yeshua had said He would rise after three days. They were afraid His disciples might steal the body and claim He had risen. So they went to Pilate, who ordered guards to secure the tomb. The stone was sealed, and soldiers stood watch. After the Sabbath, at dawn on the first day of the week, the two women went to the tomb. Suddenly, a strong earthquake shook the ground. An angel of Yah came down from heaven, shining brightly, and rolled the stone away. The guards trembled in fear. The angel said, "Do not be afraid. Yeshua is not here; He has risen. Go and tell His disciples." The women hurried away with both fear and great joy. On their way, Yeshua met them, and they bowed at His feet in worship. Meanwhile, the guards reported everything to the chief priests, who paid them to say that the disciples had stolen the body. Later that evening, Yeshua appeared to His disciples, but Thomas was not with them. When they told him Yeshua was alive, he said he would not believe unless he saw the marks in His hands and side. Eight days later, Yeshua appeared again while Thomas was there. When Thomas saw Him, he finally believed.

5. Let's discuss:

1. What was today's story about?
2. Where did Joseph and Nicodemus place Yeshua's body?
3. Why did the chief priests and Pharisees ask Pilate to guard the tomb?
4. What happened at dawn on the first day of the week?
5. What did the angel tell the women?
6. Who did the women meet on their way to see the disciples?
7. What did the chief priests do when the guards told them what had happened?
8. Who doubted that Yeshua had risen from the grave?

6. Activities:

* Worksheet: First of the firstfruits
* Worksheet: Sheaf of the firstfruits
* Coloring page: The sheaf of the firstfruits
* Bible word search puzzle: He is risen!
* Let's learn Hebrew: Bikkurim
* Creative writing: Firstfruits in Jerusalem
* Worksheet: Altar of burnt offering
* Bible craft: Temple treasures
* Coloring worksheet: The guards report

* Worksheet: Bribing the guards
* Worksheet: Did you know?
* Coloring page: The saints
* Bible crossword puzzle: The cross and empty tomb
* Map activity: From doubt to belief
* Bible quiz: The resurrection
* Worksheet: Timeline to resurrection

First of the firstfruits

Jerusalem was a busy city during the Feast of Unleavened Bread. Read Matthew 28, John 20, and the article below. Then answer the questions.

Jerusalem in spring was crowded with Israelites for the Feast of Unleavened Bread. According to Yah's commands in Leviticus 23:9-14, the Israelites were also preparing for the Firstfruits offering. The city usually held about 80,000 to 100,000 people, but during this Feast, some historians say as many as 500,000 pilgrims came. They traveled from Galilee, Egypt, Babylon, and Asia Minor, bringing lambs for the Temple.

It was during the week leading up to the Feast of Unleavened Bread that Yeshua rode into the city on a young donkey while Israelites waved palm branches and shouted with joy. A few days later, He was crucified on the same day the Passover lambs were killed. Three days and three nights after His crucifixion, He rose again. The tomb was empty, and Mary from Magdala, Mary the mother of James, and Salome were among the first to see that He had risen. The Apostle Paul later called Yeshua "the firstfruits of those who have fallen asleep" (1 Corinthians 15:20).

At the same time, the priests were holding the Firstfruits Ceremony at the Temple. The night before, workers cut the first ripe barley from a field near the city. Using torches to see, they cut one sheaf, tied it, and carried it to the Temple. This sheaf was called the omer. At sunrise, the high priest lifted the omer and waved it before Yah, thanking Him for the new crop and asking Him to bless the rest of the harvest. This ceremony was accompanied by the burning of a perfect male lamb as a burnt offering, along with a grain offering of fine flour mixed with oil and a drink offering of wine. No one could eat new grain until this ceremony was complete. It was on this same morning that Yeshua rose from the grave.

1. Why did so many Israelites travel to Jerusalem in springtime?

2. Explain the Firstfruits Ceremony.

3. What happened to Yeshua on the same day as the Firstfruits Ceremony?

Sheaf of the firstfruits

Read Leviticus 23:9-12 (ESV). Using the words below, fill in the blanks to complete the Bible passage.

| YAHWEH | HARVEST | SABBATH | LAMB | FIRSTFRUITS |
| ISRAEL | OFFERING | SHEAF | MOSES | PRIEST |

"…………………… spoke to ……………………, saying, "Speak to the children of …………………… and tell them, 'When you have come into the land which I give to you and reap its ……………………, then you shall bring the sheaf of the …………………… of your harvest to the ………………… and he shall wave the sheaf before Yah, to be accepted for you. On the next day after the ………………… the priest shall wave it. On the day when you wave the …………………, you shall offer a male …………………… without defect a year old for a burnt ………………… to Yah."

"...you shall bring the sheaf of the firstfruits of your harvest to the priest."

(Leviticus 23:10)

He is RISEN!

Read Matthew 28, Mark 16, Luke 24, John 20, and Acts 1.
Find and circle the words below.

```
S E G U A R D S Y M M K F N X
F T A X I B I U Q J E K B X N
I I O R Z G R X R H S F B Y C
P C R N T G E W H R S Y R G L
S O P S E H H V N J I J I A P
Y N C I T G Q H F E A E S R V
R C N R Y F M U M C H R E D U
Y Y J S K G R K A D Z U N E A
F E J U E W V U R K W S G N N
T Z S R Y S K G I O E A Z D G
Q A S H B W S Z B T B L Y Q E
U S U B U A B W J F S E F A L
J M E S H A O X F D I M Y R K
A P P O I N T E D T I M E S X
D I S C I P L E S Z V Z T Q S
```

RISEN
GUARDS
MESSIAH
FIRSTFRUITS
STONE
GARDEN
JERUSALEM
DISCIPLES
EARTHQUAKE
ANGEL
YESHUA
APPOINTED TIME

Bikkurim

The Hebrew name for "firstfruits" is Bikkurim. During the Firstfruits Ceremony in ancient Israel, the Israelites brought the first produce of their spring harvest and offered it to Yah. As part of the ceremony, the priest waved the first sheaf of barley, called the omer, before Yah at the Temple as a thanksgiving offering. The Bible records that Yeshua rose from the grave on the same morning the Firstfruits offering was presented.

Bikkurim
בִּכּוּרִים

Firstfruits

Trace the Hebrew name here:

בִּיכוּרִים

בִּיכוּרִים

Write the Hebrew name here:

Let's write!

Practice writing the word 'Bikkurim' on the lines below.

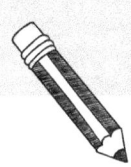

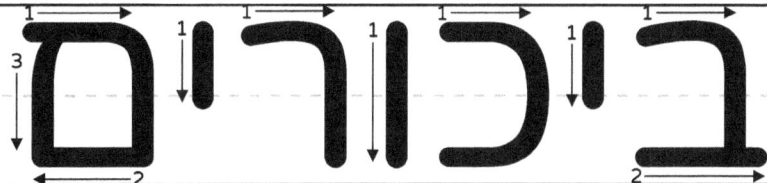

בִּכּוּרִים

Try this on your own.
Remember that Hebrew is read from RIGHT to LEFT.

_____

_____

Why do you think the apostle Paul called Yeshua the "firstfruits," and how does this connect to the Firstfruits Ceremony?

....
....
....
....

Write a story

Imagine you are an Israelite at the Temple on the day Yeshua rose from the grave. Describe the Firstfruits Ceremony and what you witnessed, including the saints who came out of their tombs, and explain what happened to Yeshua on the same morning.

....
....
....
....
....
....
....
....
....

Altar of Burnt Offering

In ancient Israel, farmers brought Bikkurim (firstfruits) to the Temple as Yah commanded. These offerings were presented near the altar of burnt offering. During the Firstfruits Ceremony, the high priest waved a sheaf of barley before Yah on behalf of the people. This barley was the first crop to ripen each year. At the time of Yeshua, the altar at Herod's Temple was large and square. It was about 10 cubits high (around five meters) and 32 cubits wide (around 16 meters).

The altar had two main parts: the altar platform and the ascent ramp. Both were made of stones and earth. On the four corners of the altar were stone projections called horns. This altar remained in place until the Romans destroyed Jerusalem in AD 70. Read more about the altar of burnt offering and the Firstfruits Ceremony in Exodus 23, 27, and 38, Leviticus 1-7 and 23, Deuteronomy 26, 2 Chronicles 4, and Ezekiel 43, then label the altar below.

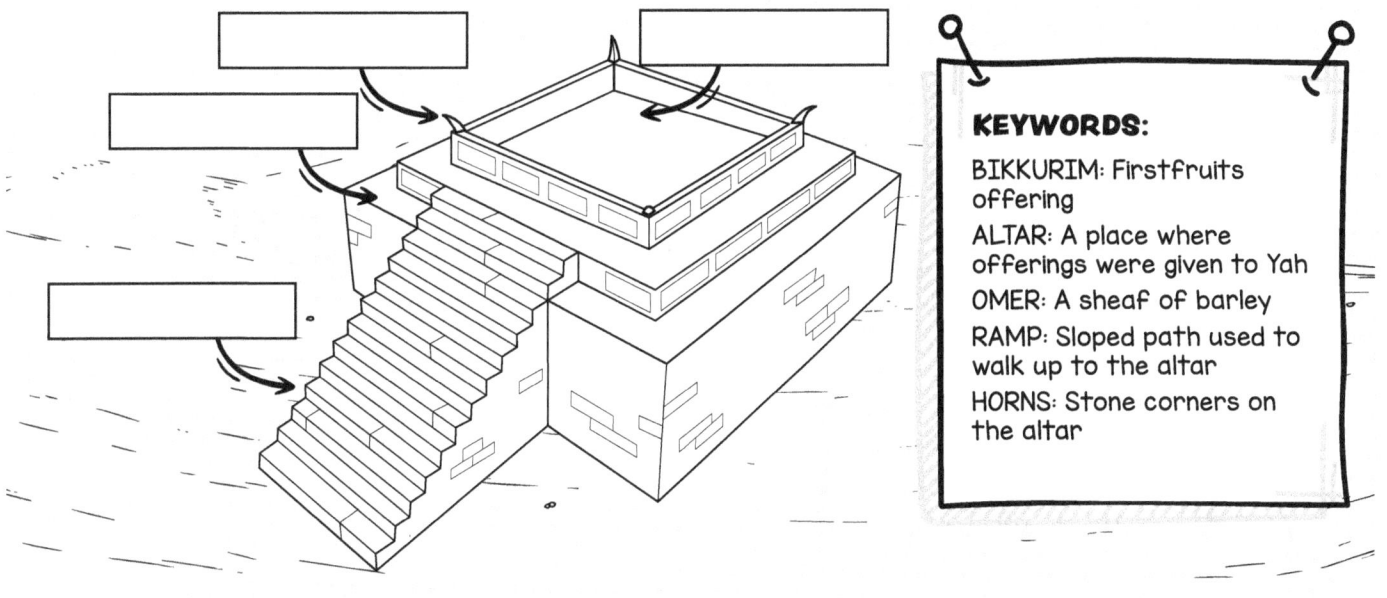

KEYWORDS:

BIKKURIM: Firstfruits offering
ALTAR: A place where offerings were given to Yah
OMER: A sheaf of barley
RAMP: Sloped path used to walk up to the altar
HORNS: Stone corners on the altar

Copy Leviticus 23:9-11 on the lines below.

....

....

....

....

The guard's report

What happened when the Roman guards told the priests the tomb was empty? Read Matthew 28 and answer the questions below. Color the soldier.

① Who told the religious leaders that Yeshua was gone?

....
....
....

② What did the religious leaders give the soldiers to keep quiet?

....
....
....

③ What did the religious leaders tell the soldiers to say about Yeshua's disappearance?

....
....
....

Bribing the guards

"You shall take no bribe, for a bribe blinds the clear-sighted and subverts the cause of those who are in the right." (Exodus 23:8)

A group of religious leaders gave Roman soldiers money to stay quiet about Yeshua's resurrection. This money was a bribe. What does it mean to bribe someone? A bribe is when you offer something, like money, to get a favor. Bribery can be a crime. For example, if someone wanted to bring a forbidden item into a country, they might offer a customs officer money to let it pass. In some places, dishonest people won't do their jobs without extra money. If people are caught taking bribes, they might lose their jobs. The Bible says bribery is wrong and tells us to be honest instead (Exodus 23:8, Proverbs 17:23, Deuteronomy 16:19).

In your own words, explain how the priests bribed the Roman guards in Matthew 28.

....
....
....
....

Draw a line to match each word to its meaning.

Bribe	Something against the law
Honesty	Money for a favor
Crime	Telling the truth

Did You Know?

After Yeshua's resurrection, some miraculous events took place. "Behold, the curtain of the temple was torn in two, from top to bottom. The earth shook, and the rocks were split. The tombs were also opened. Many bodies of the saints who had fallen asleep were raised, and coming out of the tombs after His resurrection, they went into Jerusalem and appeared to many" (Matthew 27:51-53).

Discuss the saints who came out of their tombs. Who were they? Then draw a scene from this Bible passage.

"**Many bodies of the saints who had fallen asleep were raised. They came out of the tombs and appeared to many.**"

(Matthew 27:52-53)

The cross and EMPTY TOMB

Read Matthew 28, Mark 16, Luke 24, John 20, and Acts 1 (ESV). Complete the crossword below.

ACROSS

5) The Roman governor who sentenced Yeshua to die.
7) This type of spiritual being opened the tomb.
8) Yeshua was crucified on this Roman device.
9) The disciple who betrayed Yeshua.

DOWN

1) What was torn from top to bottom inside the temple?
2) Who came out of their tombs and appeared to many?
3) Name of the place where Yeshua was crucified.
4) Yeshua met his disciples by this sea.
5) This disciple jumped out of the boat and swam to Yeshua.
6) After Yeshua died, this shook the city.

From doubt to belief

Thomas did not believe Yeshua was alive. What changed his mind? Read John 20 and answer the questions.

① What did Thomas need to see to believe that Yeshua had risen?

....

....

② How many days after His resurrection did Yeshua appear to the disciples?

....

....

③ What did Yeshua do to help Thomas believe that He had risen from the grave?

....

....

④ Read Luke 24. In which city did Yeshua first appear to His eleven disciples after He rose from the grave? Circle the city on the map.

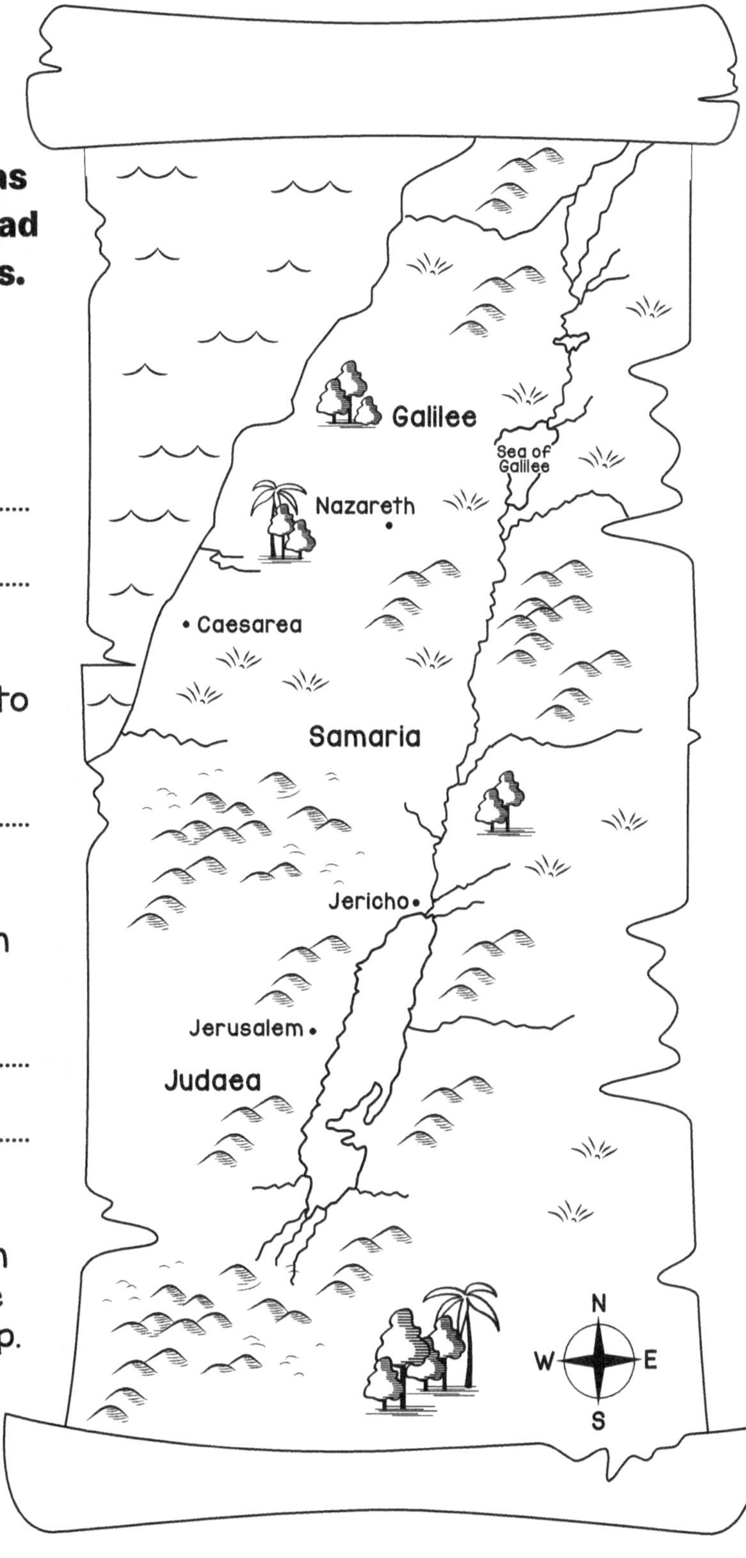

The RESURRECTION

**Read Matthew 28, Mark 16, Luke 24, and John 20.
Answer the questions below.**

1. Who rolled away the stone from Yeshua's tomb?

2. Who were the first people to find out that Yeshua had risen?

3. What did the priests give the Roman guards to keep quiet?

4. Which woman met Yeshua outside the tomb?

5. When Mary from Magdala, Mary the mother of James, and Salome went to the tomb with their spices, what did they find?

6. What did the two strangers say to the women outside the tomb?

7. Which disciple doubted that Yeshua was alive?

8. When Peter and John ran to the tomb, what did they see inside?

9. What did Yeshua say when He appeared to His disciples in the locked room?

10. What did Yeshua show Thomas to prove He was alive?

Timeline to resurrection

First, read Matthew 27, Mark 15, Luke 23 and John 19. Then, read each clue and write the Bible verse(s) that describe these events in the empty box below.

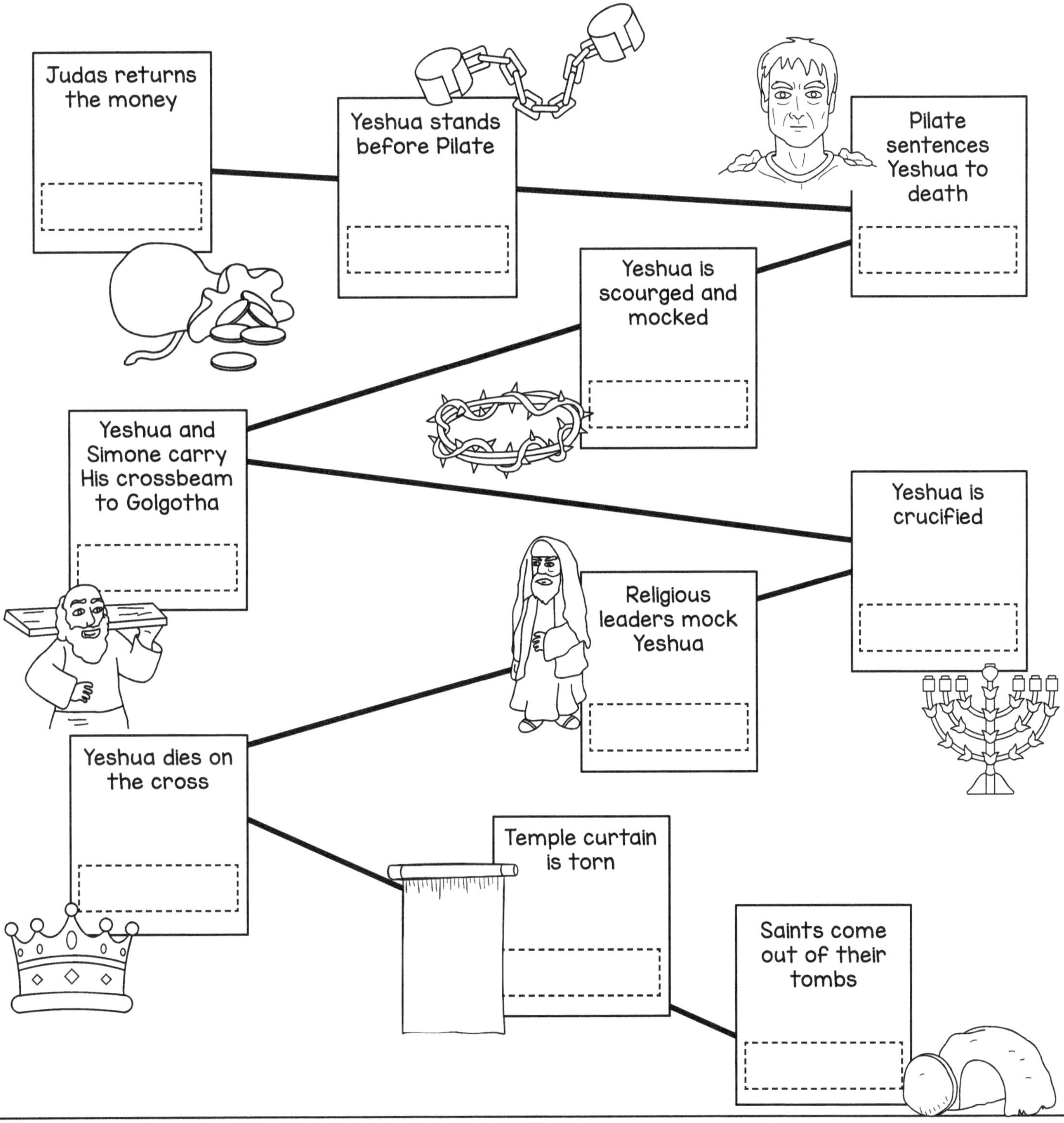

- Judas returns the money
- Yeshua stands before Pilate
- Pilate sentences Yeshua to death
- Yeshua is scourged and mocked
- Yeshua and Simone carry His crossbeam to Golgotha
- Religious leaders mock Yeshua
- Yeshua is crucified
- Yeshua dies on the cross
- Temple curtain is torn
- Saints come out of their tombs

Yah's Covenant with Abraham, Isaac, Jacob… and You!

Yah made a promise, called a covenant, with Abraham and his descendants. He promised to give them the land of Canaan, make them into a great nation, bless them, and be their Elohim forever. He passed this promise to Isaac and then to Jacob, who was also called Israel. In Exodus 6:2-4, He reminded Moses of this covenant, saying, "I appeared to Abraham, to Isaac, and to Jacob, as El Shaddai… I also established my covenant with them to give them the land of Canaan."

Create a paper chain to show how God's covenant connects one generation to the next, like a strong chain that represents the House of Israel and never breaks.

Instructions:

1. Color and cut out the strips on the next page. Write your name on the blank strip.
2. Glue the ends of one strip together to make a loop.
3. Place the next strip through the first loop before gluing it.
4. Keep repeating this step to form a chain. Then hang your chain in your home or classroom to remember that God always keeps His promises.

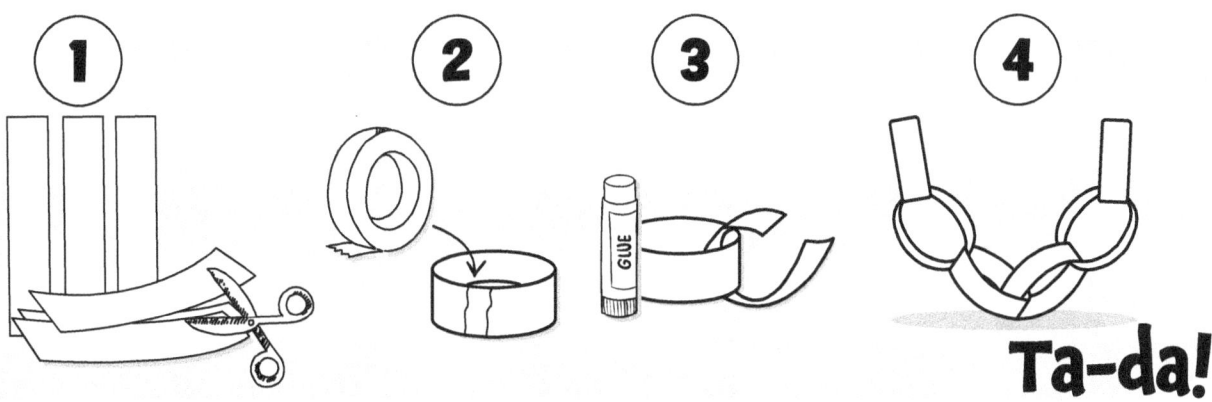

Bible Pathway Adventures

✏️ Optional extra:

On the back of each strip, write one of the promises Yah made to Abraham and his descendants, such as giving them the land of Canaan, making them into a great nation, blessing all families of the earth through them, or being their Elohim forever (Genesis 12-13, 17-18, and 22).

- Abraham
- Isaac
- Jacob (Israel)
- Moses
- Yahweh

Create your own Passover lamb

Yah told the Israelites to prepare a lamb for the first Passover meal. They were to choose a spotless lamb and mark their doorposts and lintel with its blood as a sign of protection (Exodus 12:1-7). Let's make your own paper plate lamb!

What you'll need:

 Paper plates.
 White cotton balls.
 Black construction paper.
 Craft animal eyes.
 School glue and scissors.

Instructions:

1. **Cut out the lamb template:** Carefully cut out the lamb template pieces before you begin.
2. **Cover the plate:** Spread school glue over a paper plate. Cover the glue with white cotton balls to create the lamb's body.
3. **Assemble the lamb:** Help your child put together the lamb's face using the template pieces and craft eyes. Glue the lamb's head and legs onto the cotton ball body.

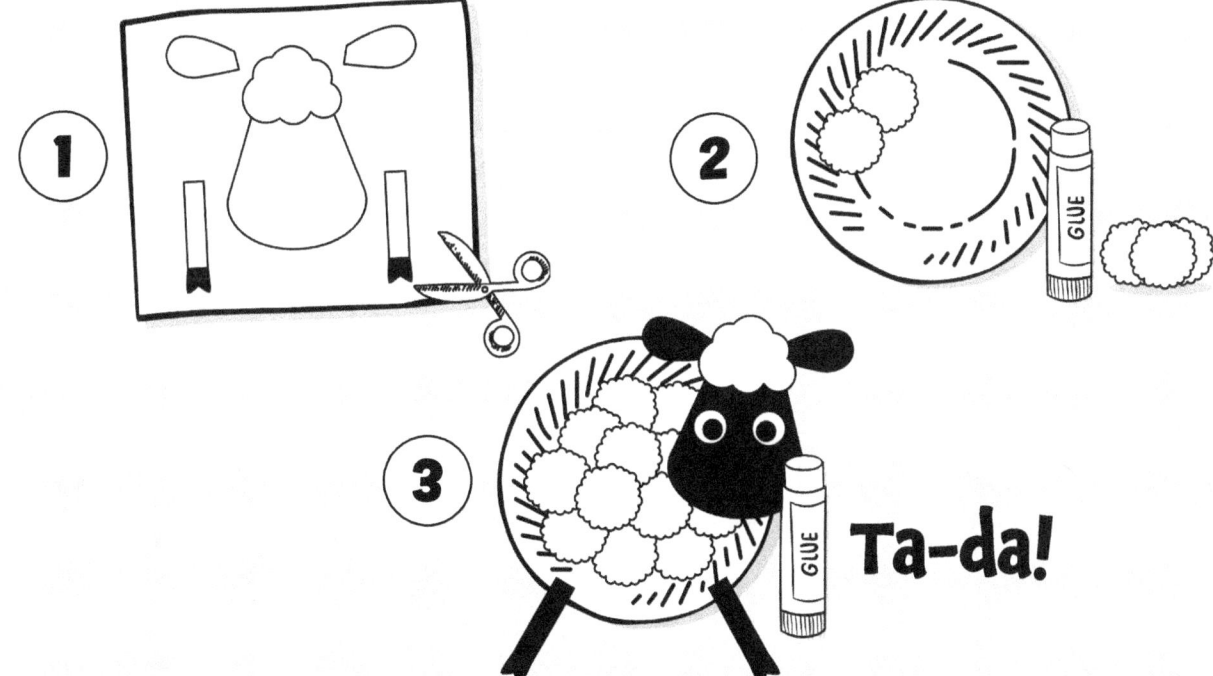

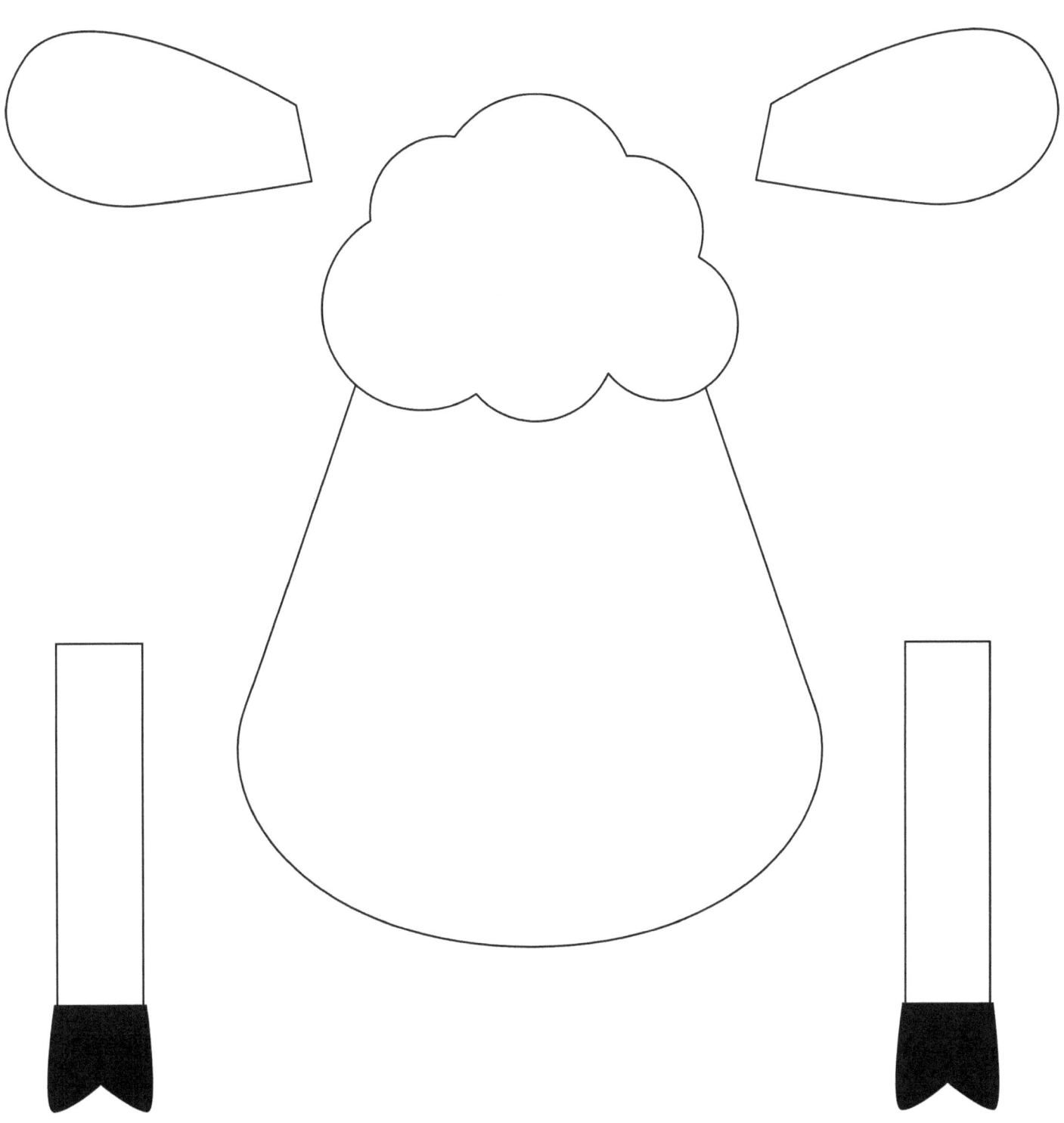

The Last Supper Fact Wheel

Cut out the two templates. Insert a paper fastener through the middle of both templates and secure. Spin the wheel and answer the questions.

The Last Supper

"This is My body, which is given for you."

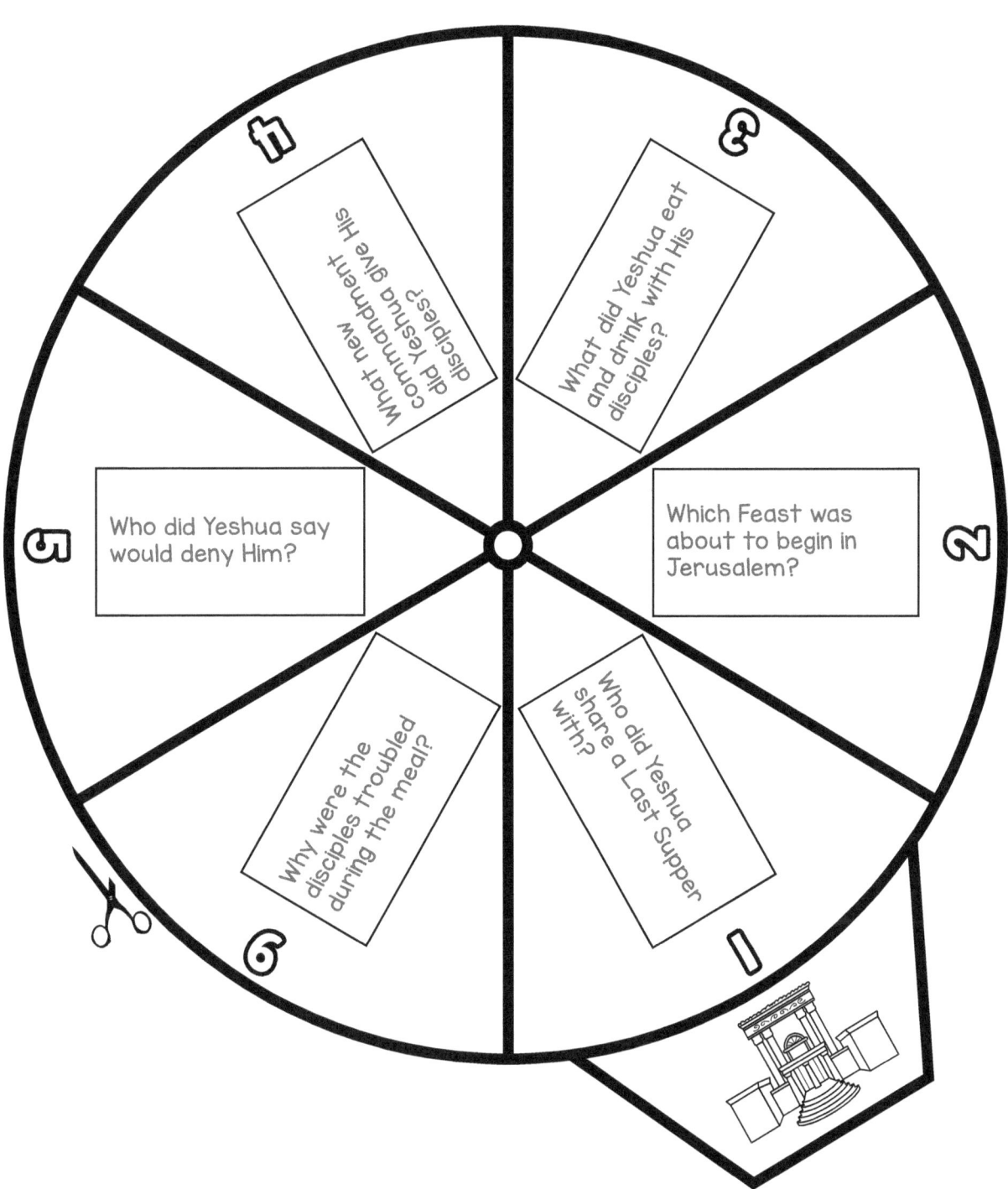

The Passover Banner craft

Yah told the Israelites to remember and honor the Passover meal forever (Leviticus 23:4-5). Let's create a Passover banner to remember your Passover meal.

What you'll need:

 Cardstock.

 Scissors and glue stick.

 Markers or Crayons.

 Stickers and drawing supplies.

 Craft stick, small piece of wood, or a ruler.

 String and tape.

Instructions:

1. Using your piece of cardstock, cut the bottom edge so it looks like a banner.
2. Cut out and color the Passover images on the next page. Paste them onto your banner.
3. Decorate around the pictures with drawings or stickers that remind you of this important meal.
4. Tape the top of your banner to a small piece of wood, a craft stick, or a ruler. Tie a piece of string to each end so you can hang your banner.

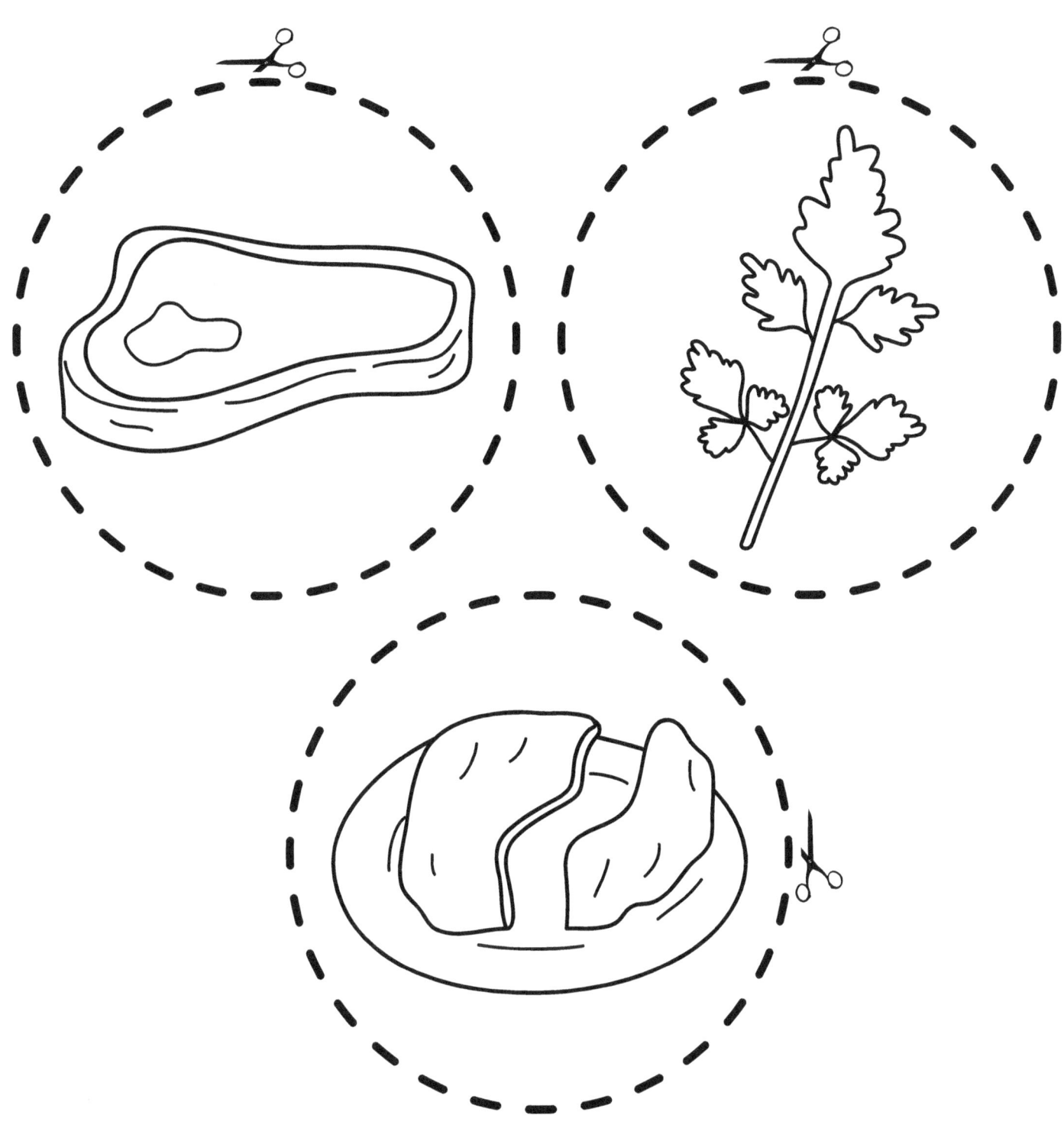

Temple treasures craft

At the time of Yeshua, the Temple in Jerusalem was the place where the Israelites came to worship Yah. Match the important Temple objects to learn what was inside the Temple. Can you explain what each object was used for?

What you'll need:

 Scissors (adults only).

 Crayons, felt pens, or colored pencils.

 School glue.

Instructions:

1. Copy or print the craft template on the next page.
2. Color and cut out the Temple objects.
3. Paste each object into the correct square on the template.

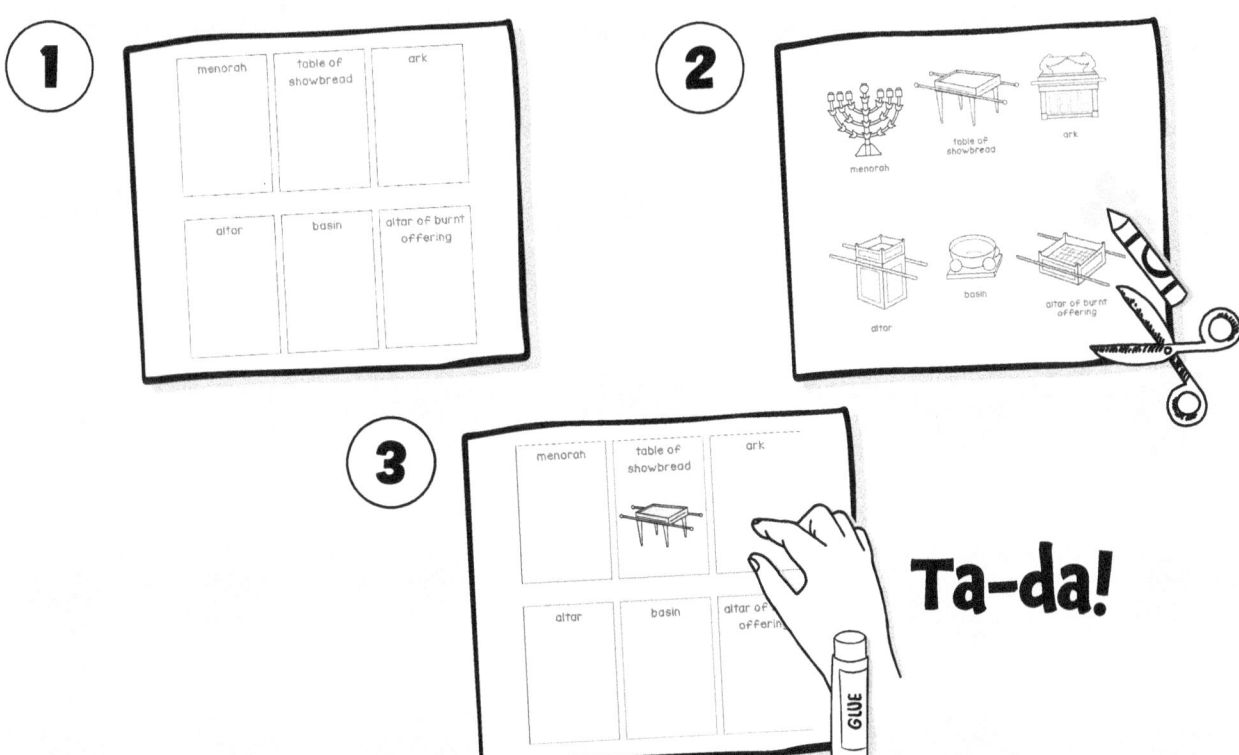

Ta-da!

menorah	table of showbread	ark
altar	basin	altar of burnt offering

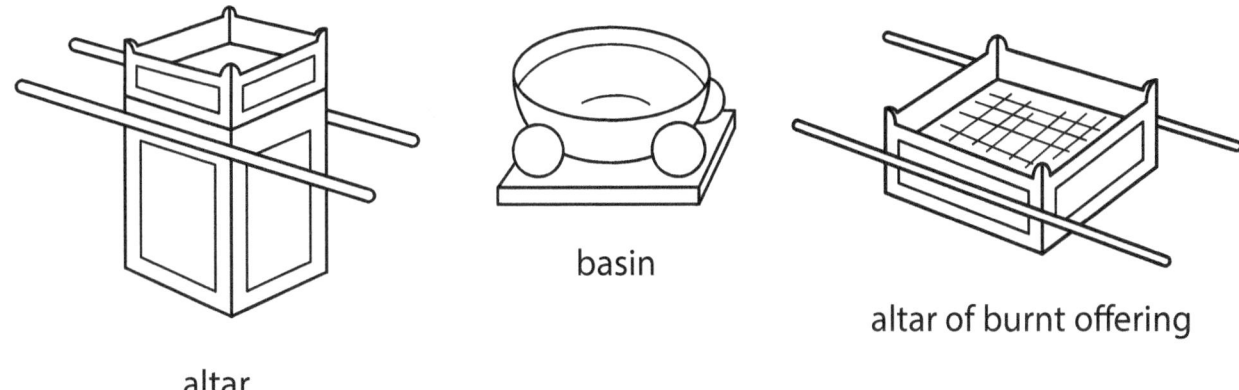

Lesson Materials Checklists

Bible Pathway Adventures

 **Lesson Materials Checklist**

Lesson One: Let My people go!

Supplies Needed:

- ☐ Bible
- ☐ Let My people go! lesson plan
- ☐ Soft sponge
- ☐ Hard rock
- ☐ Crayons or markers, and pencil(s)
- ☐ Atlas or internet for map of Egypt
- ☐ Scissors
- ☐ Stick glue
- ☐ Green pom poms *(optional)*
- ☐ Toy frogs *(optional)*
- ☐ Orange and yellow tissue paper *(optional)*
- ☐ Flashlights *(optional)*
- ☐ Dark sheets *(optional)*

Materials to Print (one for each student):

- ☐ Worksheet: Hebrew slaves in Egypt
- ☐ Map activity: Where is Egypt?
- ☐ Worksheet: Who was Moses?
- ☐ Worksheet: Let My people go!
- ☐ Bible craft: Yah's covenant
- ☐ Coloring page: Out of slavery
- ☐ Bible quiz: Let My people go!
- ☐ Math worksheet: Plagues math challenge
- ☐ Worksheet: Decode the hieroglyphics
- ☐ Role-play worksheet: Plagues of Egypt
- ☐ Worksheet: Yah's plague power
- ☐ Story sequencing activity: Plagues of Egypt
- ☐ Worksheet: Land of Goshen
- ☐ Creative writing: Hebrews in the land of Goshen
- ☐ Worksheet: Light in Goshen
- ☐ Let's learn Hebrew: Mosheh

My notes:

....
....
....
....

Lesson Materials Checklist
Lesson Two: The First Passover

Supplies Needed:

- [ ] Bible
- [ ] The First Passover lesson plan
- [ ] Picture or drawing of doorframe *(from a book or the Internet)*
- [ ] Crayons or markers
- [ ] Pencil(s)
- [ ] Small twig or leafy branch
- [ ] String or thread
- [ ] Small bowl or paper plate
- [ ] Red acrylic craft paint
- [ ] Cardstock and a paper plate (one per student)
- [ ] White cotton balls
- [ ] Black construction paper
- [ ] Craft animal eyes
- [ ] School glue
- [ ] Scissors
- [ ] 1 cup flour
- [ ] 1/3 cup vegetable oil and 1/8 tsp. salt
- [ ] 1/3 cup water and a bowl
- [ ] Spoon and fork
- [ ] Parchment paper and baking tray
- [ ] Oven

Materials to Print (one for each student):

- [ ] Bible activity: The Hebrew calendar
- [ ] Worksheet: Yah's instructions for Israel
- [ ] Worksheet: Let's inspect the lamb!
- [ ] Coloring page: The Passover
- [ ] Worksheet: Protected by the blood
- [ ] Did you know? Blood of the lamb
- [ ] Let's learn Hebrew: Pesach
- [ ] Worksheet: A Passover meal
- [ ] Worksheet: A Passover invitation
- [ ] Bible craft: Create your own Passover lamb
- [ ] Bible quiz: The first Passover
- [ ] Bible puzzle: The Feast of Unleavened Bread
- [ ] Worksheet: Feast of Unleavened Bread
- [ ] Recipe: Let's make matzah!
- [ ] Let's learn Hebrew: Matzah
- [ ] Bible word search puzzle: Feast of Unleavened Bread
- [ ] Creative writing: The Exodus escape
- [ ] Worksheet: The Exodus begins
- [ ] Coloring page: Leaving Egypt…

Lesson Materials Checklist

Lesson Three: The Last Supper

Supplies Needed:

- [ ] Bible
- [ ] The Last Supper lesson plan
- [ ] Leavened bread *(if not teaching this during the Feast of Unleavened Bread)*
- [ ] Unleavened bread
- [ ] Crayons or markers
- [ ] Pencil(s)
- [ ] Scissors
- [ ] Paper fastener

My notes:
....
....
....
....

Materials to Print (one for each student):

- [ ] Worksheet: Feast of Unleavened Bread
- [ ] Worksheet: Triumphal Entry
- [ ] Worksheet: Interview a disciple
- [ ] Comic worksheet: Cleansing the Temple
- [ ] Bible quiz: The Last Supper
- [ ] Bible word search puzzle: The Master's last meal
- [ ] What's the Word: Blood of the Covenant
- [ ] Coloring page: Do this in remembrance of Me
- [ ] Worksheet: The upper room
- [ ] Bible word unscramble: The twelve disciples
- [ ] Worksheet: Yeshua and the Twelve
- [ ] Worksheet: Steps of Discipleship
- [ ] Bible puzzle: A renewed commandment
- [ ] Worksheet: Final instructions
- [ ] Creative writing: Write a story
- [ ] Bible craft: The last supper

Lesson Materials Checklist

Lesson Four: Betrayal of the King

Supplies Needed:

- [ ] Bible
- [ ] Betrayal of the King lesson plan
- [ ] Picture of an olive branch or olive trees *(from a book or the internet)*
- [ ] Crayons or markers
- [ ] Pencil(s)
- [ ] Highlighter two different colors *(optional)*

My notes:
....
....
....
....

Materials to Print (one for each student):

- [ ] Worksheet: Yah's Appointed Times
- [ ] Worksheet: Sabbath to Sukkot
- [ ] Bible story worksheet: Betrayal of the king
- [ ] Worksheet: 30 pieces of silver
- [ ] Did you know? worksheet: Judas' betrayal
- [ ] Worksheet: Freedom from Roman rule
- [ ] Bible quiz: Garden of Gethsemane
- [ ] Worksheet: Betrayal in the garden
- [ ] Worksheet: Watch and pray
- [ ] Worksheet: Yeshua on trial
- [ ] Worksheet: Before the Sanhedrin
- [ ] Worksheet: Caiaphas, the high priest
- [ ] Story sequencing activity: Sequence the story
- [ ] Math worksheet: Unleavened math challenge
- [ ] Let's learn Hebrew: Feast of Unleavened Bread
- [ ] Worksheet: Preparation Day in Jerusalem
- [ ] Worksheet: Preparation Day chart

Lesson Materials Checklist

Lesson Five: The Crucifixion

Supplies Needed:

- [ ] Bible
- [ ] The Crucifixion lesson plan
- [ ] Crayons or markers
- [ ] Pencil(s)
- [ ] Scissors
- [ ] Stick glue
- [ ] Cardstock
- [ ] Stickers and drawing supplies
- [ ] Craft stick, small piece of wood or a ruler
- [ ] String and tape

My notes:
....
....
....
....

Materials to Print (one for each student):

- [ ] Coloring worksheet: Yeshua before Pilate
- [ ] Bible crossword puzzle: Pontius Pilate
- [ ] Coloring page: Walking to Golgotha
- [ ] Worksheet: Journey to Golgotha
- [ ] Newspaper worksheet: The Jerusalem Times
- [ ] Coloring worksheet: Your Passover meal
- [ ] Worksheet: The Passover Lamb
- [ ] Bible quiz: The Crucifixion
- [ ] Creative writing: The Crucifixion
- [ ] Worksheet: Betrayal and the cross
- [ ] Worksheet: The Passover meal
- [ ] Worksheet: Into the tomb
- [ ] Coloring page: Into the tomb
- [ ] Worksheet: Passover in Jerusalem
- [ ] Bible quiz: Feast of Unleavened Bread
- [ ] Coloring worksheet: The centurion's statement
- [ ] Bible craft: Make a Passover banner

Lesson Materials Checklist

Lesson Six: He is Risen!

Supplies Needed:

- [ ] Bible
- [ ] He is Risen! lesson plan
- [ ] Small box or jar decorated to look like a tomb *(optional)*
- [ ] Crayons or markers
- [ ] Pencil(s)
- [ ] Scissors
- [ ] Stick glue

My notes:
....
....
....
....

Materials to Print (one for each student):

- [ ] Worksheet: First of the firstfruits
- [ ] Worksheet: Sheaf of the firstfruits
- [ ] Coloring page: The sheaf of the firstfruits
- [ ] Bible word search puzzle: He is risen!
- [ ] Let's learn Hebrew: Bikkurim
- [ ] Creative writing: Firstfruits in Jerusalem
- [ ] Worksheet: Altar of burnt offering
- [ ] Bible craft: Temple treasures
- [ ] Coloring worksheet: The guards report
- [ ] Worksheet: Bribing the guards
- [ ] Worksheet: Did you know?
- [ ] Coloring page: The saints
- [ ] Bible crossword puzzle: The cross and empty tomb
- [ ] Map activity: From doubt to belief
- [ ] Bible quiz: The resurrection
- [ ] Worksheet: Timeline to resurrection

Answer Key

Lesson One: Let My people go!
Let's discuss:
1. Today's Bible story was about how God sent nine plagues on the land of Egypt
2. Moses and Aaron went to Pharaoh to tell him to let the Hebrews go and worship God
3. Pharaoh refused to obey God and would not let the Hebrews go
4. God sent the plagues to show Pharaoh His power, so that His name would be proclaimed throughout the earth
5. The first nine plagues were water turned to blood, frogs, gnats, flies, livestock disease, boils, hail, locusts, and darkness
6. The Hebrews lived in the land of Goshen during the plagues
7. God protected the Hebrews by keeping the land of Goshen separate from the plagues in Egypt
8. Ask students to answer this question. Answers may vary

Worksheet: Hebrew slaves in Egypt
1. Pharaoh made the Hebrews slaves because he was afraid they were becoming too numerous and might join Egypt's enemies
2. Pharaoh told the midwives to kill all Hebrew baby boys at birth
3. Moses' mother hid him in a basket in the Nile River

Worksheet: Who was Moses?
1. Pharaoh's daughter adopted Moses
2. After Moses killed an Egyptian, he fled to the land of Midian
3. Yah's powerful signs included turning his staff into snake, and turning Moses' hand leprous
4. God sent Moses back to the land of Egypt to free the people of Israel
5. Moses had two sons: Gershom and Eliezer
6. Ask students to answer this question. Answers may vary

Bible quiz: Let My people go!
1. Yah sent Moses and Aaron to speak to Pharaoh
2. Moses and Aaron told Pharaoh to let the Hebrews go so they could worship Yah
3. Pharaoh refused to obey and would not let the Hebrews go
4. Pharaoh forced the Hebrews to make bricks without straw
5. Yah sent plagues to show His power so that His name would be proclaimed throughout all the earth (Exodus 9:16)
6. The first plague was the Nile River turning to blood
7. The Hebrews lived in the land of Goshen

8. Yah reminded Moses of His covenant with Abraham, Isaac, and Jacob, promising to give their descendants the land of Canaan as an everlasting inheritance.
9. Moses warned that the firstborn in every Egyptian household would die
10. Yah promised to protect the Hebrews and bring them out of slavery

Math worksheet: Plagues math challenge
1. **River of Blood:** When Yah turned the Nile River to blood, it lasted for 7 days.
   Each day, the Egyptians used 20 jars of water from other sources. $7 \times 20 = 140$ jars. Answer: 140 jars of water
2. **Plague of frogs:** One frog laid 200 eggs, and there were 15 frogs near a single home. $15 \times 200 = 3{,}000$ eggs. Answer: 3,000 eggs
3. **Fiery hail:** Fiery hail destroyed 800 fields of grain. Each field had 125 bundles of wheat. $800 \times 125 = 100{,}000$ bundles: Answer: 100,000 bundles of wheat destroyed

Worksheet: Decode the hieroglyphics
1. Yah said he would bring the <u>children of Israel</u> out of Egypt

Worksheet: Yah's plague power
1. **Plague of Blood**
   - **Yahweh Says START:** "Stretch out your staff over the rivers and streams..." (Exodus 7:19)
   - **Moses STOPS IT:** Moses prayed to Yahweh, and the water became clean again. (Exodus 8:11)
2. **Plague of Frogs**
   - **Yahweh Says START:** "Stretch out your hand with your staff over the streams and pools..." (Exodus 8:5)
   - **Moses STOPS IT:** Moses asked Yahweh to take away the frogs, and they died. (Exodus 8:12-13)
3. **Plague of Gnats**
   - **Yahweh Says START:** "Strike the dust of the ground so it becomes gnats..." (Exodus 8:16)
   - **Moses STOPS IT:** There is no stop command. The magicians said, "This is the finger of God." (Exodus 8:18-19)
4. **Plague of Flies**
   - **Yahweh Says START:** "Go to Pharaoh and say, 'Let my people go... or I will send swarms of flies.'" (Exodus 8:20-21)
   - **Moses STOPS IT:** Moses prayed to Yahweh, and the flies were gone. (Exodus 8:30-31)

5. **Plague of Darkness**
   - **Yahweh Says START:** "Stretch out your hand toward the sky, so there will be darkness..." (Exodus 10:21)
   - **Moses STOPS IT:** Moses lifted his hand, and darkness came. Later, Pharaoh said they could leave. (Exodus 10:22-23)

Story sequencing activity: Plagues of Egypt
1. Moses and Aaron told Pharaoh that God said to let the Hebrews go, but Pharaoh refused.
2. Pharaoh made the Hebrews work harder by forcing them to find their own straw for bricks.
3. Yahweh decided to send ten plagues to show His power over Pharaoh and the Egyptian gods.
4. The first plague turned the Nile River into blood, killing the fish and making the water undrinkable.
5. The second plague brought frogs everywhere, filling the Egyptians' homes.
6. God sent lice and flies, causing trouble throughout Egypt.
7. The fifth plague brought sickness to the Egyptian animals, but the Hebrews' animals were unharmed.
8. God sent boils, hail with fire, and locusts to ruin Egypt's crops and health.
9. Another plague covered Egypt in darkness for three days, but the Hebrews had light in the land of Goshen.

Worksheet: Land of Goshen
1. The Hebrews came to live in the land of Egypt, in the land of Goshen, while Joseph was a ruler of Egypt (Genesis 45-46)
2. At first, the Hebrews were shepherds in the land of Goshen. Later, they became slaves and were forced to make bricks and build cities
3. Bible verses include: Genesis 46:28, 47:1, Exodus 8:22, 9:26

Lesson Two: The First Passover
Let's discuss:
1. Today's Bible story was about the first Passover in the land of Egypt, when Yah protected the Israelites and led them out of slavery
2. Yah told each family to choose a one-year-old male lamb without blemish, and at twilight on the fourteenth day, the lambs were killed as part of the Passover meal
3. The lamb's blood was placed on the doorposts and lintel as a sign so Yah would pass over the houses and protect the Israelite families inside
4. Yah protected the Israelites by passing over their homes when He saw the blood on the doorposts
5. The Israelites were told to eat the Passover meal in haste because they needed to be ready to leave the land of Egypt
6. The Israelites left Egypt with silver, gold jewelry, and clothing because Yah gave them favor in the eyes of the Egyptians

7. The Feast of Unleavened Bread is a seven-day feast, also called an Appointed Time, that reminds the Israelites they left the land of Egypt quickly without time for their bread to rise
8. When the Israelites entered the land of the Canaanites, they were commanded to set apart their firstborn to Yah and to teach their children that Yah brought them out of Egypt with a mighty hand after Pharaoh refused to let them go

Bible activity: The Hebrew calendar

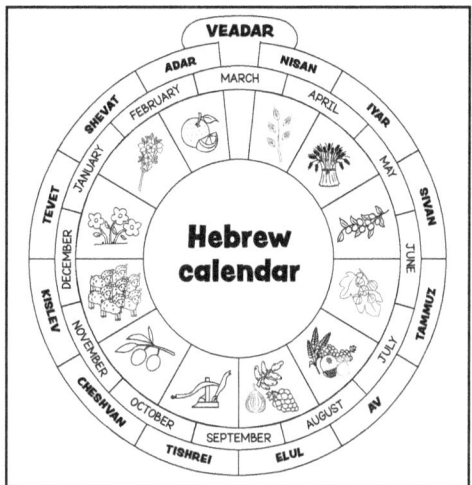

Worksheet: Yah's instructions for Israel
1. **Passover food:** Yah told the Israelites to eat roasted lamb, not raw or boiled. Along with the lamb, they were to eat unleavened bread (matzah) and bitter herbs (Exodus 12:8-9). They were not to leave any leftovers until morning, and if any food remained, they had to burn it (Exodus 12:10)
2. **Choosing the lamb:** Each household was required to take a lamb for their Passover meal (Exodus 12:3). If a family was too small to eat a whole lamb, they were to share with a neighbor (Exodus 12:4). The lamb had to be a one-year-old male without defect, and it could come from either the sheep or goats (Exodus 12:5). The Israelites were to take care of the lamb until the 14th day of the month, when they would slaughter it at twilight (Exodus 12:6)
3. **Marking with blood:** After slaughtering the lamb, the Israelites were instructed to take some of its blood and put it on the sides and top of the doorframe of their houses (Exodus 12:7). This act would serve as a sign of protection, ensuring that when God passed through Egypt to strike down the firstborn, He would pass over the homes marked with blood and no harm would come to them (Exodus 12:13)
4. **Eating the meal:** The Israelites were commanded to eat the meal quickly, with their cloaks tucked into their belts, sandals on their feet, and staffs in their hands (Exodus 12:11)

Bible quiz: The first Passover
1. The Israelites were told to put lamb's blood on the doorposts and lintel of their houses

2. The Israelites were told to sacrifice a male one-year-old lamb without blemish
3. The Israelites put lamb's blood on the sides and top of the doorframe (doorposts and lintel) of their houses
4. The blood protected the Israelites from the death of the firstborn during the final plague
5. The Israelites ate roasted lamb, unleavened bread, and bitter herbs for the Passover meal
6. The Israelites were told to observe the Feast of Unleavened Bread for seven days, forever
7. The Israelites were told not to eat anything with yeast during the Feast of Unleavened Bread
8. The firstborn of every Egyptian household, including animals, died during the final plague
9. Pharaoh told Moses and the Israelites to leave Egypt immediately after the final plague
10. The Israelites packed quickly, took their possessions and dough (before it was leavened), and left the land of Egypt

Bible puzzle: Feast of Unleavened Bread
1. Seven: 19-5-22-5-14
2. days: 4-1-25-19
3. you: 25-15-21
4. shall: 19-8-1-12-12
5. eat: 5-1-20
6. unleavened: 21-14-12-5-1-22-5-14-5-4
7. bread: 2-18-5-1-4

Worksheet: Feast of Unleavened Bread
1. Unleavened bread is bread made without yeast, so it doesn't rise and stays flat. The Israelites made unleavened bread when they left Egypt because God told them to leave quickly. They didn't have time to let their bread rise, so they baked it without yeast
2. Ask students to answer this question. Answers may vary
3. Ask students to answer this question. Answers may vary

Bible word search puzzle: Feast of Unleavened Bread

Worksheet: The Exodus begins
1. At midnight, Yah struck down all the firstborn in Egypt, and Pharaoh finally told the Israelites to leave
2. The Israelites took their flocks, herds, unleavened dough, and the silver, gold, and clothing given to them by the Egyptians
3. The mixed multitude likely included Egyptians and other foreigners who left the land Egypt with the Israelites

Lesson Three: The Last Supper
Let's discuss:
1. Today's Bible story was about Yeshua traveling to the city of Jerusalem, clearing the Temple, and eating a final meal with His disciples
2. Many Israelites traveled to Jerusalem to honor the annual Feast of Unleavened Bread
3. Many Israelites welcomed Yeshua by waving palm branches and praising Yah as He entered Jerusalem
4. The chief priests and scribes were worried because they feared the people and Yeshua's influence
5. Yeshua saw money changers and merchants doing business in the Temple, and He drove them out
6. Yeshua shared a final meal to teach His disciples, serve them, and prepare them for what was coming
7. Ask students to answer this question. Answers may vary
8. Yeshua gave a new commandment to love one another as He had loved them

Worksheet: Triumphal Entry
1. Yeshua sent two of His disciples into the village to find a young donkey and a colt for Him to ride
2. The prophecy from Zechariah 9:9 was fulfilled, saying Israel's King would come riding on a donkey
3. The Israelites welcomed Yeshua by waving palm branches, spreading their cloaks on the road, and shouting praises to Yah

Bible quiz: The Last Supper
1. Yeshua and His disciples at a meal in the upper room, also known as the Upper Room in Jerusalem
2. Yeshua and His disciples ate bread and drank wine at the meal
3. Yeshua washed the feet of His disciples
4. Judas Iscariot left the meal to betray Yeshua
5. Yeshua gave the new commandment to love one another as He has loved them
6. Yeshua said Peter would deny Him three times
7. A dispute arose among the disciples about who would be the greatest
8. If we love the Messiah, we will keep His commandments. (John 14:15)
9. The Holy Spirit (Ru'ach), whom Yeshua called the Helper, would teach them all things

10. After the meal, Yeshua took the disciples to the Garden of Gethsemane on the Mount of Olives

Bible word search puzzle: The Master's last meal

Worksheet: Blood of the Covenant
On the first day of the Feast of Unleavened Bread, when it was customary to sacrifice the Passover lamb, Yeshua's disciples asked Him, "Where do you want us to go and make preparations for you to eat the Passover?" He sent two of His disciples, telling them, "Go into the city, and a man carrying a jar of water will meet you. Follow him. Say to the owner of the house he enters, 'The Master asks: Where is My guest room, where I may eat the Passover with My disciples?' He will show you a large room upstairs, furnished and ready. Make preparations for us there." The disciples left, went into the city and found things just as Yeshua had told them, and prepared the Passover. When evening came, Yeshua arrived with the Twelve. While they were reclining at the table eating, He said, "Truly I tell you, one of you will betray Me - one who is eating with Me." They were saddened, and one by one they said to Him, "Surely you don't mean me?" "It is one of the Twelve," He replied, "one who dips bread into the bowl with Me. The Son of Man will go just as it is written about Him. But woe to that man who betrays the Son of Man! It would be better for him if he had not been born." While they were eating, Yeshua took bread, and when He had given thanks, He broke it and gave it to his disciples, saying, "Take it; this is My body." Then He took a cup, and when He had given thanks, He gave it to them, and they all drank from it. "This is My blood of the covenant, which is poured out for many," He said to them. "Truly I tell you, I will not drink again from the fruit of the vine until that day when I drink it new in the kingdom of God."

Bible word unscramble: The twelve disciples
Peter, Andrew, James, John, Philip, Bartholomew, Matthew, Thomas, James (son of Alphaeus), Jude, Simon, and Judas Iscariot

Worksheet: Steps of Discipleship
1. Learned the Torah in a community setting
2. Asked a Teacher to become his disciple
3. Evaluated by the Teacher
4. Received an invitation to "Follow me"
5. Left home and daily work
6. Traveled with his Teacher
7. Learned by watching and listening
8. Imitated his teacher's way of life

Bible puzzle: A renewed commandment
1. Love: 12-15-22-5
2. one: 15-14-5
3. another: 1-14-15-20-8-5-18
4. as: 1-19
5. I: 9
6. have: 8-1-22-5
7. loved: 12-15-22-5-4
8. you: 25-15-21

Worksheet: Final instructions
1. Yeshua said that we show we love Him by obeying His commandments (John 14:15)
2. Some bible scholars believe that Judas betrayed Yeshua because he was disappointed that He had not overthrown the Roman rulers. Judas believed that by arranging Yeshua's arrest, he could force Yeshua to reveal Himself as the next king of Israel
3. Yeshua taught the disciples about the importance of obeying Yah's commands, servanthood, the coming of the Holy Spirit, hatred of the world, and that He was the true vine

Lesson Four: Betrayal of the King
Let's discuss:
1. Yeshua and His disciples went to the Garden of Gethsemane so He could pray and prepare for His arrest
2. Yeshua prayed that Yah's will would be done, even though He knew He would go to His death
3. Judas betrayed Yeshua by accepting thirty pieces of silver and leading soldiers to Him, identifying Him with a kiss
4. The disciples ran away when Yeshua was arrested. Peter followed at a distance and later denied knowing Yeshua while in the courtyard
5. The religious leaders wanted to arrest Yeshua because they were threatened by His teachings and authority
6. Caiaphas was the high priest and leader of the Sanhedrin
7. The Sanhedrin found Yeshua guilty by using false witnesses and accusing Him of blasphemy
8. Yeshua was sent to Pilate because the Sanhedrin did not have the authority to put Him to death

Worksheet: 30 pieces of silver
1. Judas was a zealot, and he may have been motivated by a desire for personal gain or a misguided belief that he could force Yeshua into taking the throne
2. Ask students to answer this question. Questions may vary
3. Judas showed the soldiers which person was Yeshua by giving Him a kiss. This was a pre-arranged signal to identify Yeshua in the garden of Gethsemane

Bible quiz: Garden of Gethsemane
1. Yeshua ate a meal with His disciples in the upper room before His arrest
2. Yeshua prayed in the Garden of Gethsemane before He was arrested
3. While Yeshua was praying, Peter, James, and John fell asleep
4. Yeshua warned Peter that he would deny Him three times
5. Judas betrayed Yeshua with a kiss in the garden
6. An angel appeared to Yeshua in the garden to give Him strength
7. The religious leaders gave Judas thirty silver coins to betray Yeshua
8. Yeshua came to Jerusalem to keep the Feast of Unleavened Bread
9. After Yeshua was arrested, the disciples ran away in fear
10. The temple guards first took Yeshua to Annas, the father-in-law of Caiaphas, the high priest. Then, they brought Him to Caiaphas and the Sanhedrin

Worksheet: Betrayal in the garden
1. Yeshua prayed three times before He was arrested: TRUE
2. The disciples stayed awake and prayed with Yeshua: FALSE
3. Judas identified Yeshua to the soldiers by shaking His hand: FALSE
4. Yeshua told Peter to put away his sword after he cut off the servant's ear: TRUE
5. An angel came to strengthen Yeshua: TRUE
6. Yeshua tried to escape but was caught by the high priest: FALSE

Worksheet: Yeshua on trial
Yeshua's trial before the Sanhedrin was unusual because it took place at night, even though the council normally met during the day. It also happened during the time leading up to Passover, when such trials were not usually held

Worksheet: Before the Sanhedrin
Those present at or near the trial that night, when Yeshua appeared before the Sanhedrin Council, included:
- Chief priests
- Caiaphas
- Servant girl
- Members of the Sanhedrin Council
- Scribes (Torah teachers)
- False witnesses
- Temple guards
- Peter

1. False witnesses claimed that Yeshua said He would destroy the Temple and rebuild it in three days, even though He was speaking about His body, not the building
2. Peter followed from a distance and waited in the courtyard, but when people recognized him, he denied knowing Yeshua three times before the rooster (Temple Crier) crowed
3. The Sanhedrin accused Yeshua of blasphemy and decided He deserved to die, then sent Him to Pontius Pilate for judgment

Worksheet: Caiaphas, the high priest
1. The temple guards first took Yeshua to Annas, the former high priest
2. Annas was the father-in-law of Caiaphas and a former high priest
3. Caiaphas asked Yeshua if He was the Messiah, the Son of God

Worksheet: Sequence the story
1. Yeshua and His twelve disciples gathered in an upper room in Jerusalem to share a final meal.
2. During the meal, Yeshua took bread, gave thanks, broke it, and said, "This is My body given for you."
3. He lifted a cup of wine and said, "This cup that is poured out for you is the renewed* covenant in my blood."
4. Yeshua told His disciples that one of them would betray Him, and Judas left the room and went into the night.
5. After singing from the Psalms, Yeshua led the disciples across the Kidron Valley to the Garden of Gethsemane.
6. In the garden, Yeshua prayed in deep sorrow while Peter, James, and John fell asleep nearby.
7. Judas arrived with soldiers and temple guards, greeted Yeshua with a kiss, and they arrested Him.
8. The disciples fled, but Peter followed at a distance to the courtyard of the high priest's palace, where he denied knowing Yeshua three times.
9. That night, the Sanhedrin met in the palace of the High Priest, Caiaphas, and accused Yeshua of blasphemy.
10. At sunrise, the council tied Yeshua up and sent Him to Pontius Pilate, the Roman governor, for judgment.

Worksheet: Unleavened math challenge
1. Removing the Leaven: 3 rooms × 15 minutes each = 45 minutes to clean the whole house
2. Baking for the Feast: 4 batches × 12 loaves per batch = 48 loaves of unleavened bread (matzah) in total
3. Feeding the Pilgrims: 400,000 pilgrims × 2 pieces per day = 800,000 pieces per day.
800,000 × 7 days = 5,600,000 pieces of matzah eaten during the Feast of Unleavened Bread

Lesson Five: The Crucifixion

Let's discuss:
1. The religious leaders brought Yeshua to Pilate because only the Roman governor had the authority to order His death
2. Pilate asked Yeshua if He was the King of the Jews and questioned Him about the religious leaders' charges against Him
3. Pilate released Barabbas because the people demanded it and he wanted to keep peace with them
4. After Pilate made his decision, Yeshua was flogged and handed over to be crucified
5. While Yeshua was on the cross, darkness covered the land, the earth shook, and the Temple veil was torn
6. After Yeshua died, the Roman centurion declared that He was the Son of God
7. Yeshua was buried before sunset because the Sabbath was approaching and work had to stop at sundown
8. Joseph of Arimathea placed Yeshua in the tomb

Worksheet: Yeshua before Pilate

Order	Event	What happened?
1	The chief priests' accusations.	The chief priests accused Yeshua of misleading the people, opposing payment of taxes to Caesar, and claiming to be the Messiah, a king.
2	What Pilate learned about Yeshua.	Pilate questioned Yeshua and found no reason to put Him to death by crucifixion.
3	The crowd's demands.	The crowd shouted for Yeshua to be crucified and asked for Barabbas to be released instead.
4	Pilate's decision.	Pilate released Barabbas and handed Yeshua over to the Roman soldiers to be crucified on a cross outside Jerusalem.

Bible crossword puzzle: Pontius Pilate

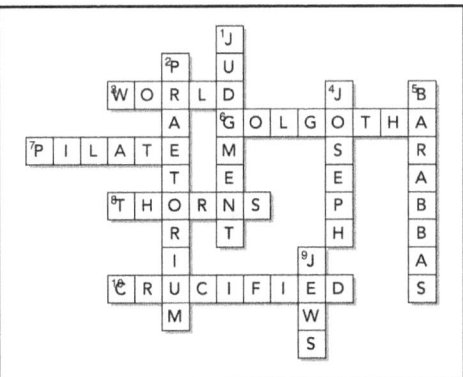

Worksheet: Journey to Golgotha
1. Pontius Pilate sentenced Yeshua to die on a cross
2. Simon of Cyrene helped carry Yeshua's crossbeam to Golgotha
3. The sign above Yeshua's head said: "King of the Jews"

Bible quiz: The Crucifixion
1. Pilate sentenced Yeshua to die
2. Simon of Cyrene was forced to carry Yeshua's crossbeam
3. Yeshua was nailed to the cross at Golgotha, outside Jerusalem
4. The sign above Yeshua's head said, "King of the Jews."
5. Yeshua cried out, "My God, My God, why have You forsaken Me?"
6. Two criminals were crucified next to Yeshua
7. Darkness covered the land for three hours after Yeshua died
8. The Roman soldier used a spear to pierce Yeshua's side
9. After Yeshua died, some of the saints who had fallen asleep came out of their tombs
10. Mary from Magdala and Mary, the mother of James and Joseph, watched Yeshua's crucifixion

Bible quiz: Feast of Unleavened Bread
1. The word 'unleavened' means bread made without yeast
2. The Feast of Unleavened Bread lasts for seven days
3. The Feast of Unleavened Bread begins on the 15th day of the month of Nisan
4. Yah told the Israelites to remove all yeast or leaven from their homes
5. The Israelites ate bread without yeast because they left Egypt in a hurry and their dough had no time to rise
6. During the Feast of Unleavened Bread, the Israelites ate flat bread called 'matzah'
7. All Israelite men were commanded to appear before Yah during the Feast of Unleavened Bread
8. In Yeshua's time, pilgrims from all over Israel and beyond journeyed to Jerusalem to celebrate the Feast together
9. In 1 Corinthians 5:8, the apostle Paul encouraged Israelites to keep the Feast of Unleavened Bread
10. After the Feast of Unleavened Bread, Paul sailed from Philippi to join his companions in Troas, where he stayed for seven days (Acts 20:6)

Coloring worksheet: The centurion's statement
1. The roman centurion said, "Truly this was a righteous man."
2. The darkness, the earthquake, and the way Yeshua died helped the centurion realize that Yeshua was the son of Yah
3. Ask students to answer this question. Answers may vary

Bible Pathway Adventures

Lesson Six: He is Risen!
Let's discuss:
1. Today's story was about Yeshua's burial, His resurrection, and how the priests tried to hide the truth of His resurrection
2. Joseph placed Yeshua's body in his own new tomb, which was carved from solid rock, and rolled a large stone in front of it
3. The chief priests and Pharisees asked Pilate to guard the tomb because they were afraid Yeshua's disciples might take His body
4. At dawn on the first day of the week, there was a great earthquake, and an angel of Yah came down, rolled back the stone, and sat on it
5. The angel told the women not to be afraid and to go tell Yeshua's disciples that He was alive
6. The women met Yeshua on the way to see His disciples
7. The chief priests paid the guards a bribe and told them to say that Yeshua's disciples had stolen His body while they were asleep
8. Thomas doubted that Yeshua had risen from the grave

Worksheet: Sheaf of the firstfruits
Yahweh spoke to Moses, saying, "Speak to the children of Israel and tell them, 'When you have come into the land which I give to you and reap its harvest, then you shall bring the sheaf of the firstfruits of your harvest to the priest and he shall wave the sheaf before Yah, to be accepted for you. On the next day after the Sabbath the priest shall wave it. On the day when you wave the sheaf, you shall offer a male lamb without defect a year old for a burnt offering to Yah.

Bible word search puzzle: He is risen!

Worksheet: Altar of Burnt Offering

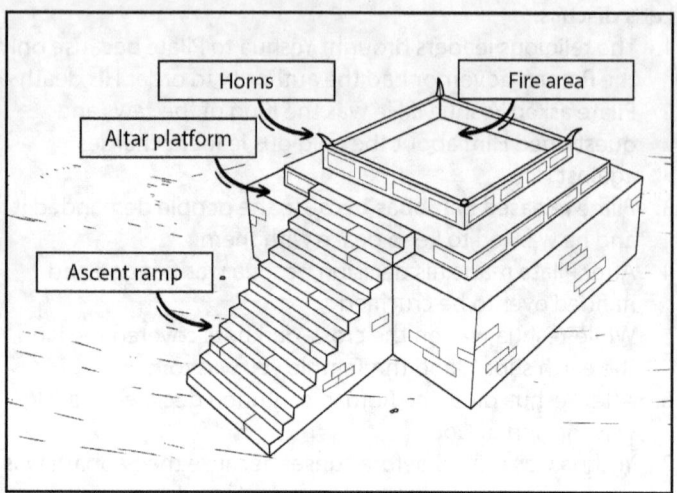

Coloring worksheet: The guards report
1. A group of Roman soldiers told the religious leaders that Yeshua was gone
2. The religious leaders gave the guards money (a bribe) to stay silent
3. The religious leaders told the guards to say that Yeshua's disciples had come by night and stolen Him while we were asleep

Worksheet: Bribing the guards
1. Bribe: Money for a favor
2. Honesty: Telling the truth
3. Crime: Something against the law

Bible crossword puzzle: The cross and empty tomb

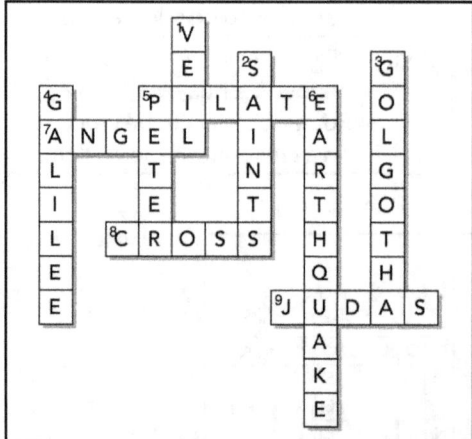

Map activity: From doubt to belief
1. Thomas needed to see the marks on Yeshua's hands and side
2. Yeshua appeared to the disciples eight days after He rose from the grave

3. Yeshua told Thomas to place his fingers on His hands, and place his hand on Yeshua's side
4. Yeshua appeared to His eleven disciples in a room in Jerusalem (Luke 24:33-37 and John 20:19)

Bible quiz: The resurrection
1. An angel of Yah rolled away the stone from Yeshua's tomb
2. Mary from Magdala and the other Mary were the first to discover that Yeshua had risen when they went to the tomb
3. The priests gave the Roman guards money (a bribe) and told them to lie, saying that Yeshua's disciples had stolen His body while they were asleep
4. Mary from Magdala met Yeshua outside the tomb
5. When Mary from Magdala, Mary the mother of James, and Salome went to the tomb with their spices, they found that the stone had been rolled away and Yeshua's body was gone
6. The two strangers told the women not to be afraid and that Yeshua had risen just as He had promised
7. Thomas, one of Yeshua's disciples, doubted that Yeshua was alive
8. When Peter and John ran to the tomb, they saw the linen burial cloths lying inside, but Yeshua's body was not there
9. When Yeshua appeared to His disciples in the locked room, He greeted them with, "Peace be with you," and showed them His hands and side
10. Yeshua showed Thomas His hands and side, and Thomas believed Him

Worksheet: Timeline to resurrection
1. Judas returns the money (Matthew 27:3-4)
2. Yeshua stands before Pilate (Matthew 27:11-14)
3. Pilate sentences Yeshua to death (Luke 23:24-25)
4. Yeshua is scourged and mocked (John 19:1-3)
5. Yeshua and Simon carry His crossbeam to Golgotha (Mark 15:21)
6. Yeshua is crucified (Luke 23:33)
7. Religious leaders mock Yeshua (Matthew 27:41-43)
8. Yeshua dies on the cross (John 19:30)
9. Temple curtain is torn (Mark 15:38-39)
10. Saints come out of their tombs (Matthew 27:52-53)

Discover more Workbooks!

 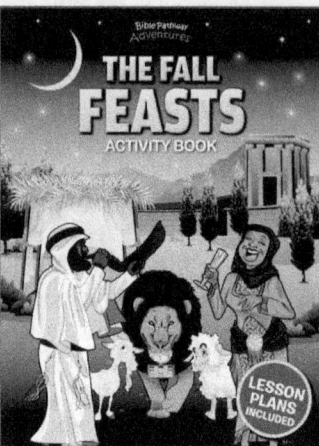  

Available for purchase at www.biblepathwayadventures.com

INSTANT DOWNLOAD!

The Fall Feasts (Beginners)
The Fall Feasts
The Spring Feasts (Beginners)
Day of Pentecost
Twelve tribes of Israel
Twelve tribes of Israel (Beginners)
He is Risen!
The Spring Feasts

www.ingramcontent.com/pod-product-compliance
Lightning Source LLC
Chambersburg PA
CBHW081429070526
44586CB00020B/2530